Going to the Dogs

Going to the Dogs

Eileen Schroeder

Illustrated by Arnie Levin

CROWN PUBLISHERS, INC.
NEW YORK

Inquiries should be addressed to Crown Publishers, Inc., One Park
Avenue, New York, New York 10016

Printed in the United States of America

Published simultaneously in Canada by General Publishing Company Limited

Library of Congress Cataloging in Publication Data

Schroeder, Eileen.
  Going to the dogs.

1. Basset-hounds—Anecdotes, facetiae, satire, etc.
2. Dogs—Anecdotes, facetiae, satire, etc.
3. Schroeder, Eileen.   I.   Title.
SF429.B2S33   636.7'53   79-23499
ISBN: 0-517-540258

Designed by Leonard Henderson

10 9 8 7 6 5 4 3 2 1
First edition

To all the dogs who have loved me

Going
to
the Dogs

INTRODUCTION

The air is so hot you strain to breathe. The dry grass crunches under your feet. You press the paper cup of tepid syrupy orange drink to your forehead, trying to cool your aching head. Waiting.

When it happens, the reaction is always the same. The adrenaline starts to flow, the excitement begins in the pit of your stomach and rolls upward until your mouth is filled with cotton. Your movements are automatic. You reach down, tighten the lead, give one final brush to an already spotless fur coat, and begin moving toward the most heart-searing, most competitive few moments in any sport man has devised for himself. Everything else is forgotten in those moments when you and your dog tell the judges and the world around you, "This is my best."

A thousand times you do it, and yet it never changes. The joy of victory, the hurt of losing—and still the anticipation is the same every time you walk through a ring gate and the judge raises his hand and says, "Take them around, please."

You just know that today you are going to win the BLUE.

1

Sitting there on the back seat, solemn-eyed, puppy fuzz askew, her tummy bulging like a pink balloon, she looked like a slightly tipsy Buddha.

Her name would be Beaucoup Bon Bones.

Future generations of her offspring would outshine her. Her few blue ribbons and one purple, her meager accumulation of Glo-Tone angels on ersatz marble bases, would be lost among the shelves of silver trophies and streamers of ribbons. But for fourteen years she would reign as the arrogant grande dame of kitchen and kennels. Nobody would ever outclass her.

Beaucoup was a most uncommon kind of Basset Hound. Family pet turned show dog. Together she and I would find our way into the wonderful, wacky world of show dogs. Smarter than I, she would learn her limitations early and retire to a life of raising puppies, chasing bunnies, and sleeping in the sun. I would turn from sensible suburban housewife into a whirling dervish of dog feeder, cleanup squad, midnight midwife, and occasionally, director of hillside burial services.

I would learn to juggle a kitchen full of hungry puppies and a dining room filled with half-starved teenagers. It keeps you active and agile. I would develop super-acute hearing trying to listen with one ear to a tearful recitation of a broken romance and with the other to the outraged wails of a mamma dog whose puppies have outgrown her.

In spite of superhuman efforts, the two worlds sometimes collided. The times, when busily dishing out the mountains of chocolate chip cookies and dog chewies that moved through my world, the distribution system went awry and the luckless recipients of my error accepted the handouts with varying degrees of enthusiasm. Neither side suffered lasting effects from the breakdowns. Proving that the addition of bone meal and charcoal to children's diets is not fatal and that dogs fed chocolate chip cookies don't suffer from increased dental caries.

To live in two worlds and keep them running side by side took a lot of humor and understanding from a family who sometimes wondered and sometimes complained, but always loved.

It would all begin on a cold, drizzly Sunday in October.

2

I don't know what ungodly hour of the morning they got up. By the time I'd staggered down the stairs at seven o'clock, they were sitting on the couch, washed, combed, coats buttoned, boots zippered. Between older daughter (eight years old, black pigtails, and red coat) and younger daughter (six years old, blonde pigtails, and blue coat) stood the empty box waiting to be filled with a new puppy.

"Get the coats off before you smother," I flung at them as I passed.

"Are you going to fool around and eat breakfast?" they groaned.

"Yes I am and so are you, and get the coats off."

"They'll all be gone before we get there."

"Nobody ever sold eleven puppies before noon on Sunday. Get the coats off."

"Boy, you sure are crabby."

It sounded like a Greek chorus.

Overhead the sky was a dirty gray. A chill October mist coated the windshield. The Illinois countryside rolled past in dreary monotony. On the back seat, the two prospective puppy owners rode silently with the empty box between them. In the suicide seat beside the driver, I juggled the map of Sangamon County and the newspaper ad that read, "PUPPIES. Healthy, farm-raised. Seven males, four females. REASONABLE."

No matter how reasonable, it still would mean macaroni-and-cheese casseroles twice a week for a month. I wondered what the heck a Basset Hound was. The tires made a singing sound on the wet road.

Please God, I prayed, let it be a nice little kind of dog.

"Can't you make her lean back in the seat? She's snotting on my neck again. I can't drive and wipe my neck too," he snapped.

"Sit back in the seat, and stop wetting your father's neck."

"I can't. She pinches me."

"You with the fingernails, quit pinching. You with the wet nose, sit back in the seat."

"Wipe the back of my neck, please."

The scuffling in the back stops. The miles roll by. We need a pit stop.

"We have to stop soon. I have to go," older daughter announces.

"No you don't," I say.

"I'll get nephritis again," older daughter threatens.

"You never had nephritis."

"The doctor said I did."

"The doctor never said that. Stop trying to be glamorous."

"I really do have to go."

"Good grief! Stop at the next Stuckey's. If you're lying, may you get nuts caught in your cavities and get a toothache."

"Boy, are you crabby."

The mist had turned into a steady, bone-chilling drizzle as we turned off the Interstate and onto a muddy, rutted country road. At the end of the road, we pulled up in front of a farmhouse that should have been abandoned twenty years before. By a three-to-one margin, I was voted most expendable. I waded through the muck toward a porch that was threatening to detach itself from the house and float away on a sea of mud. I banged on the door and waited for it to collapse inward. It opened a crack, and a shower of wet leaves from someplace fell on my head.

"May I please come in and see your puppies?" I asked. I wasn't sure, but I thought I heard a grunt from behind the door before it closed.

While I brushed off the wet leaves, I warily watched the ice box at the other end of the sagging porch. If it started my way, I was going to set a new world's record for the broad jump. The door opened again, and a lanky figure popped out like a tom cat going courting. With me trailing behind, we rounded the house, and I noticed a back porch with an even worse sag. I'd never seen a house that sagged so much and didn't fall down.

We sloshed across the chicken yard eyed by a couple of

bedraggled Rhode Island Reds from the hen-house doorway, then through a gully of waist-high weeds, detoured *around* a pig house, thank God, and wound up at a greasy, blackened fence surrounding the barnyard.

"That's them over there," he said, pointing across a reasonable facsimile of Okefenokee swamp toward a barn that looked like a death trap if I ever saw one.

"I don't see anything," I said.

"Just wait, it'll move," he said.

If anything moves out there, it would be mentally deranged, I thought. I kept looking, straining through the rain that was coming down like the first day of the deluge. Something did finally move. It raced through the mud, leaped, did a perfect Immelmann, rolled out, and headed back for the barn.

Ringing in my ears were my final instructions: "Pick a cute one, Mom."

My taciturn companion came to life again. "Thaten's a good one, mam."

My God, how could he tell? "Could I see it up close, please?"

"You gonna buy it? I don't like to bring 'em out in this weather, lessen you gonna buy."

"Well, I most certainly am not going to buy if I can't see what it looks like," I retorted.

A shrill whistle cut across the barnyard, and out of the barn came the mud ball again, racing across the field to the fence.

"That the only one you've got?" I asked.

"Only one what'll come out today," he answered.

From beneath his yellow slicker, he pulled a piece of torn feed sack and wiped off enough mud to prove it was a puppy. All I could see were two enormous floppy ears, feet that looked like bell clappers, and the softest, warmest brown eyes, which stared straight into my heart. Mud and all I took her in my arms and walked slowly back to the car.

"She was the cutest one in the bunch," I lied.

3

Anytime the phone rings at nine in the morning it's:

A. *The school nurse.* "Your son Jere thinks he's swallowed his spacer."

"It's not mine," I deny. "I only have girls."

"It's still in its snow suit. Wait, I'll check." (I always knew we'd be haunted for naming a girl with a boy's name.)

"It says it's a girl. Would you please look in her box of caterpillar cocoons before we send her home. She thinks she might have left it in there."

"What box of cocoons?"

"She says the one behind her ant farm."

"What ant farm? It broke and I threw it out a month ago."

"She says she brought it back in. It's under her bed." (No wonder we have ants in the breadbox.)

B. *My mother-in-law.* She ran the cards last night, and Junior (the father of my children) is going to have trouble with his stomach. The nine of clubs came up three times. The nine of clubs means stomach trouble.

"How is he eating?" she asks.

"With a shovel, but if the outlook is bad, I'll make him put it back outside and eat with a fork," I josh.

Where Junior is concerned, my mother-in-law doesn't josh.

"He looked peaked when you were here last Sunday. Does he still eat his hot oatmeal every morning?"

"Winter and summer," I swear.

"With brown sugar?"

"Sometimes."

"He should eat brown sugar all the time. White sugar makes pimples."

9

"If I see any pimples, I'll take his white sugar away," I promise.

I grab the receiver. "Hello."

"Hello. This is Della Mae Mertz of the City of the Arch Kennel Club calling."

"Who?" It's very hard to hear anyone over the roar of my 1932 Hoover vacuum cleaner.

"This is Della Mae—— I hear a lot of roaring. Is this a private residence?" the voice demands.

"Hang on a moment until I unplug the vacuum," I shout into the phone.

It may seem odd that I don't just reach over and flip the *off* switch, but the switch is permanently broken in the *on* position. For two years I have floundered from room to room leapfrogging over chairs, hanging over beds, unplugging the vacuum every time I have to stop for a nature call or for pots boiling over on the stove. Two years of frantic complaints have fallen on deaf ears.

With male patience and deep soul sighs, the head of the household has explained to me the intricacies of vacuum cleaners. The model I am fortunate enough to own is the second best one the Hoover Company ever made. Except for the 1929 model, now impossible to buy because the owners refuse to part with them, the '32 is unbeatable.

"I'll part with mine," I volunteer.

"You'd be sorry."

"Then buy a new switch."

"I can't. They stopped making parts for your model in 1946."

"Isn't it dangerous with electricity loose in the handle?"

"Not if you keep your hands and feet dry."

"I'll remember not to vacuum the bathtub."

I whip the cord out of the plug, and the roar dies down.

"Hi, I'm back," I yell into the phone, forgetting the monster has been defanged.

"I can hear you just fine," the caller says. "Do you have a Basset Hound?"

"Yes, I do, but she's behind the refrigerator right now. She's afraid of the vacuum." So am I, but I don't tell the caller this.

"I'll go get her if you'll wait."

"That isn't necessary. I just want to ask you a few questions."

"Are you with the health department?" I want to know.

"Certainly not." The caller sounds huffy.

"Rabies control?"

"No. I'm with the City of the Arch Kennel Club. We want to invite you to show your Basset Hound at our Puppy Fun Match this coming Sunday."

"Is it a party for puppies?" I ask, confused at the turn of events.

Della Mae Mertz is very patient with me.

"It's like a dog show, but it's not really a dog show." Now that made sense. If you know what a dog show is. Which I didn't.

"Would you explain it a little more?" I queried.

"It's all very simple. I'll ask you a few questions and put the information on an entry form; you send me $2, and I'll call you sometime Saturday and tell you when to come. Now that's easy, isn't it?"

I nodded my head at the phone and answered Della Mae's questions. Then I had a few of my own. Like what did we do when we got to the puppy party? How many guests was she expecting? Could any dogs come? I had some neighbors, maybe we could get up a car pool?

Della Mae's patience was infinite.

"No, dear, it isn't really a party. It's a sort of dog show. What kinds of dogs do your neighbors have?" she inquired hopefully.

"Oh, all different kinds," I gushed. "White ones, black ones, multicolored ones."

"No, dear. Are they purebreds?" she asked delicately.

"You mean did they have matching parents? Some of them did, I think, but some of them are thoroughbreds," I said in a display of my knack for collecting trivia.

"Oh no, dear. There are no thoroughbred dogs. There are only purebreds, those with AKC-certified parents. The others are called mixed breeds. Of course, we love them all," she hastened to assure me, lest I think her a snob.

"In that case I don't think they can come," I said, feeling a bit snobbish myself.

11

Her instructions didn't sound too complicated for the newly discovered snobbish owner of a puppy who got invited to an "almost dog show."

First I would have to buy a collar and a leash, something she pronounced lead. I knew just where I could get a peachy one— red leather with silver studs and a matching red leather leash. I didn't mention this to Della Mae; I'd surprise everybody with the flashiest dog in the show. Next I would have to walk around with her with the leash around her neck. Boo wouldn't like that. We were still carrying her around because she disliked moving under her own steam except at meal times. (Later I learned she wasn't unusual. This is a characteristic of Basset Hounds. They consider rolling over to scratch as exercise.) Also, I was told, she would have to stand still while the judge examined her. That was easy. She was immobile 99 percent of the time anyway. Della Mae's final instruction nearly finished Boo's career before she was launched.

"She must be bathed. Judges don't like soiled dogs," she said.

"But she hates water," I protested. "She won't even drink it." It was true. I explained her peculiar habits to Della Mae.

"She only drinks warm milk and the dregs from the bottom of glasses after we have a party. She's been swacked three times since we've had her. We're trying to taper her off." I got the feeling from Della Mae's answer that she was beginning to regret her invitation.

"Drinking is not good for dogs," said Della Mae sanctimoniously. "It could cause kidney trouble later."

"I know. It's not too good for people either," I agreed, "but I'll make sure she doesn't drink before the show." I must have set her fears to rest.

"We'll look forward to seeing you both on Sunday; and oh, by the way, dear, do you bake? Cakes, pies, sweet rolls? Maybe you make potato salad or mustaccioli?"

I'm confused. When she filled out the entry form, she didn't tell me I had to pass a cooking test to come to a dog show.

"Yes I can bake, and my husband says my potato salad is better than his mother's." I hope I'm passing the test.

"Then, dear, would you mind bringing your very favorite cake as a donation for the cake raffle? We try to make a little on the side to cover our expenses."

This was beginning to sound like the Boltonville Volunteer

Firemen's summer pig roast, but I agreed to bring my three-layer choco-marsh with nuts and maraschino-cherry filling to the party.

"Oh that sounds yummy, dear, and don't forget, send the two dollars right away."

When I became treasurer of the City of the Arch K.C. five years later, I found out they had $7,000 in the kitty. Cake raffles were big business for City of the Arch K.C.

I went hunting for Beaucoup to tell her the good news.

"Boo, come out from behind the refrigerator. We have to go shopping right away. Guess what, honey? You're going to a party Sunday. How's that hit you?"

While I had her attention, I thought I might as well give her the bad news, too.

"There's another thing. You're going to have to stop drinking right now. It's bad for your kidneys."

She made a puddle in the middle of the floor to prove her kidneys were working just fine.

My great news for Sunday's outing received mixed reviews from the group. Two votes in favor, father and I. Two votes against, daughters. The ayes took it by brute force.

4

I'm setting the alarm for four o'clock. You don't have to get up," I said.

"For God's sake why? I told you I'd drive you to the show," he said.

At one o'clock I asked, "Did you fill the gas tank?"

"Ummm."

At two o'clock I asked, "Are the snow tires on the car?"

"Is it snowing?" he inquired.

"No."

At three o'clock I asked, "Have you got quarters for the toll gate?"

"Ummm."

I wasn't nervous.

At four o'clock I crawled out of bed.

At five o'clock Beaucoup was tubbed. Uncooperative, but I overcame.

At six o'clock Beaucoup was very angry.

At seven o'clock Beaucoup was back in the sack. Still angry.

At eight o'clock I tubbed.

At nine o'clock our pilot announced: "Our ETA (estimated time of arrival) is 10:42 A.M. There will be no food in transit and no pit stops."

"Then I better go back in the house," older daughter announced.

"Our new ETA will now be 10:46 A.M.," the pilot revised.

Wondrous changes had been wrought in the mud ball. Her black fur shone like a polished night sky, her white turned silvery in sunlight, and her few tan marks had deepened into a rich russet. The ears hung in velvety folds, the feet had stopped growing long enough for the rest of her to catch up. Only the eyes had never changed. From under her wrinkled forehead, they looked out at the world, wise and solemn and with more love than a lifetime could contain.

We pulled up in front of a sign that said,

PUPPY FUN MATCH TODAY

Another hand-lettered sign over the door said, "Exhibitors Only."

That's me, that's me, I chortled to myself.

For fifty-cents admission, they let my nonexhibitor entourage enter through the same door. It took a bit of the glow away.

Inside was a canine Woodstock, only noisier. Dogs, dogs, dogs. Big ones, little ones, fuzzy ones, smooth ones. Overweights and boney ones. Elegantly arrogant ones and sneaky-looking sleazy ones. And they all barked. Steadily, continuously, like the hounds of hell in a butcher shop.

I made my way through the clouds of chalk dust and flying dog hair to the only human being who wasn't scraping, pulling, or spraying VO-5 Extra Hold or sugar water on her beast.

"Hello," I said. "I'm the Basset Hound."

"Hey Lucille, the Basset Hound's here," it yelled.

"Tell the Basset Hound to get in Ring Three," a disembodied voice called from somewhere behind the cloud of dust and flying hair.

"Don't you want to know who I am?" I asked plaintively.

"We don't use names at dog shows," it rebuked me.

"Then would you just point me in the direction of Ring Three, please."

"It's over there next to the hot dog machine and the ladies toilet." I was dismissed, as the voice went back to counting tickets.

On the way over to the hot dog machine and the ladies toilet, two Scotties tried to remove Beaucoup's head. She stepped in a giant-sized pile of very wet dog feces. One Alaskan Malamute tasted my ankle, and two fifteen-inch Beagles nearly deflowered Boo before I booted their hind legs out from under them. Slightly the worse for wear, we arrived at Ring Three. I noticed my entourage was more interested in the hot dog machine than in my upcoming debut.

15

A prim-looking little lady in a crocheted hat and white gloves snapped a hunk of cardboard with a number on it around my arm, made a check mark in her book, lit a cigarette, and yelled in a raucous voice that didn't fit the hat and gloves, "Okay, Edna; it's here."

One hundred seventy-five pounds of flowered crepe de chine materialized in front of me, waved an arm loaded with rattlely gold bracelets, and said, "Take her around."

"Which way?" I peeped.

"Counterclockwise," it said in a voice that implied I was a dummy for asking.

I was eight years old before I quit saying, "Mom if the big hand is on three and the little hand is on nine, what time is it?"

Which way is counterclockwise?

I went the wrong way. Crepe de chine caught me on the second clockwise circuit and put me out of my misery.

"Stand over there," crepe de chine said.

I followed an inch-long "Cherries in the Snow" fingernail to over there.

The ceremony was brief but tasteful, as the saying goes. Crepe de chine handed me a pink ribbon with gaudy gold lettering that said "First Prize" and a six-inch naked angel on a blue ersatz marble base.

I floated past white gloves, past the same two fifteen-inch Beagles waiting with the same gleam in their eyes, past the hot dog machine, and into the arms of my waiting entourage. Now that they were fed, they were interested.

"Didja win, mom?" younger daughter asked ingratiatingly. There were two hot dogs still left in the machine.

"Of course," I said, smug in victory.

"Heck, Boo was the only one in there," older daughter deflated. She gets gas from hot dogs.

"Our ETA is 11:57 A.M. There will be no food in transit and no pit stops," the pilot announced.

This time he meant it. The football game started at 2:00 P.M.

I returned in triumph from the contest with my ribbon and my naked angel. I had the best Basset Hound in the show.

Della Mae Mertz, wherever you are: Thank you for starting me.

17

5

Boo and I were becoming fixtures at City of the Arch K.C. incessant puppy fun matches. We were sort of their live-in Basset Hound entry. But I was learning.

In the ten months since that first pink ribbon, I had learned, among other things, that five out of nine judges had a vision problem. I had met most of the poor-sighted ones by the time I left for the greener fields of real dog shows and my string of victories began to wane (Boo was no longer the only Basset contestant). I was also learning the lingo. "Stacking your dog" meant posing it for a judge to examine. The well-trained ones stood like carved marble. I achieved limited success because most of mine through the years leaned, slumped, jiggled, or simply fell over on their sides. Another characteristic of my chosen breed.

I learned, too, that you didn't walk your dog around the ring, you "gaited." In my case gaiting meant galumphing around the ring at a pace somewhere between a leisurely stroll and Secretariat coming down the home stretch. It depended on how interested Boo was in the dog in front of her. And I learned that dog shows are a stronghold of male chauvinism. Not all dogs are dogs. Only males are called dogs; females are called bitches. It took a while before I stopped choking everytime I called poor Boo a bitch.

Still over the horizon were other things. Dog crates, those wire or wooden contraptions used to transport valuable dogs to shows. Tack boxes, which are makeup kits for dogs. Whelping boxes for lady dogs who are in a family way. And a veterinarian, with whom I would spend more after-midnight hours than with anyone else besides my spouse.

To date my score wasn't exactly the thing they write books

about. I had three pink ribbons and three naked angels (City of the Arch K.C. seemed to have an unending supply of six-inch naked angels); I'd made three donations—two choco-marsh cakes and a half-gallon of my best potato salad; and I'd had a heck of a shock.

I'd discovered after the third angel and my third donation that those pink ribbons from puppy fun matches didn't count for anything except to impress non-purebred dog owners and kids' friends. On top of that shocking revelation, I'd found that crepe de chine Edna wasn't a real judge. Very few judges at puppy matches ever are. Edna was a member of the faithful who alternated between judging and running the cake raffle at City of the Arch K.C.'s shows. Her know-how about Basset Hounds was practically zilch.

Finding out that Edna didn't know a heck of a lot more than I did about Basset Hounds cast a slight pall over the glow from the pink ribbons and angels. Two of them were from Edna, and the third wasn't too soul-satisfying, either. Edna's replacement was another of the faithful who alternated between judging and running the soda concession. C. of A.'s judging panel was multitalented. I guess if Boo hadn't finally passed the age limit for puppy doings, I'd still be trading choco-marsh cakes for Glo-Tone angels.

In January, exactly fifteen months after our first match, Boo and I went big time. We sailed on a tide of pink ribbons into the world of blue ribbons, championship points, and real judges.

I should have stuck with crepe de chine Edna and C. of A. At least they appreciated my culinary skill.

By May, six shots at the big time added up to:

1. 6 entry fees @ $5.00 each (1960 prices).
2. 83 gallons of gasoline @ $.36 per gallon.
3. 12 half-cooked hot dogs and watery orange drink lunches @ $1.25. (The kids had opted for grandma's roast beef and stringbeans after the third pink-ribbon outing.)
4. 6 baths on 6 successive Saturdays for Boo, who was beginning to challenge me every time she saw the tin tub coming out.

And the football season was coming around again.

So far my efforts had garnered:

1. 1 blue ribbon. We were the only Basset Hound entry.
2. 5 red ribbons. We were one of two Basset Hound entries.

3. 1 slightly disgruntled husband.

Today was the last straw! "That does it," I muttered, as we made our way toward the entrance.

"What are you going to do now?" the assistant bather, furnisher of money for entry fees, and still husband inquired.

I strode across the parking lot, yanked the car door open, boosted Boo onto the back seat, and made the announcement that would set me on the course for the next twenty years.

"I'll tell you what I'm going to do," I said. "I'm going to breed one of my own. That's what I'm going to do."

"Oh!"

6

Boo was getting on my nerves.

Six months had dragged by after my declared intention to breed a good one of my own, and nothing was happening.

A check with the veterinarian had revealed that normally a bitch comes "in season," as it is delicately put, somewhere between ten and fourteen months of age. I was not to worry. There were exceptions. I had an exception.

We celebrated her eighteen-month birthday with great enthusiasm, hoping to gently jog her along toward a little cooperation in making herself available for motherhood. She enjoyed her birthday party immensely, lapping up her bowls of ice cream, accepting the extra petting with wags for everybody, but she still showed no signs of interest in sex and motherhood. I couldn't understand her.

Besides being raised on threats and nightly doses of cod liver oil during the colds' season, I'd also somehow acquired the idea that all lady dogs produced puppies at the sight of a male dog. Perhaps it came from hearing my mother's constant warnings: "Don't bring another female around here. All they do is have puppies."

My mother would have loved Boo.

More time passed. It was October again. Boo's two-year birthday party featured plain vanilla ice cream, which was all I thought she deserved. At the rate she was holding out, I would be on Social Security before I made good on my promise. She was maddening.

For an entire year, I had seen more of Boo's backside than I had of her face. The longer she held out, the more frantic became my checks. We looked like we were on the opposite sides of a seesaw. Every time she stood up, I bent over and looked. Twice a week I had to pumice my knees for the calluses I was growing, crawling around on the floor behind her. We made umpteen visits to the vet, and umpteen times he'd assure me she was a normal, healthy female, except for this one small (to him) flaw. She was sickening, standing there on the examination table chewing on her vitamin-enriched chewy cookies while he poked around and pronounced her perfectly capable of conceiving.

"She'll come around one of these days," he'd console as I shuffled out of the office.

"Listen you," I'd yell at her on the ride home. "Do you think that just because you've got a couple of pink ribbons and some sleazy angels you're going to sit around on your duff for the rest of your life?"

A couple of times I could have sworn she gave me a sort of smug grin, but she was probably picking chewy cookie out of her teeth.

It was February, she was close to twenty-eight months old, and I was convinced I owned the only permanent virgin in the dog kingdom. A few discreet inquiries among friends who had lady dogs turned up the fact that I owned a very unusual dog. I didn't need an unusual dog. I needed a mother dog.

We quit going to the vet. I quit checking her bottom. I started raising the lemon trees I got from coffee coupons. The lemon trees did splendidly. At least I could grow something.

March the third will go down in the family records along with marriages, births, and deaths.

Everyone else had scattered to school or to work, and Boo and I were alone in the kitchen. While I finished up my last cup of coffee, she sat waiting for her handouts: half a sausage link from the plate of younger daughter, who never liked meat; crusts of toast from the plate of older daughter, who didn't eat crusts; most of the egg from the plate of father, who didn't like his eggs runny. Nothing from me. I'd licked the platter clean.

"Okay," I said. "If you want it you're coming over here to get it. I'm not walking over to you." I held the half a sausage link down to her. She raised herself and walked across the three feet of floor that separated us, took her sausage, and chewed it thoroughly (Boo never gulped anything). I was reaching for the toast crust when my eyes spotted something where she'd been sitting. Trying not to get my hopes up, I told myself one of the kids had spilled ketchup or they were making cherry Kool-Aid out of season.

"Turn around, Boo. Let me see your backside," I ordered. She had had a lot of experience with my examinations and was in no hurry to cooperate. She never did approve of my meddling in her private business.

"Don't sit down on it, dummo. I want to see it." I boosted her to her feet, swung her around, and bent over. It had finally happened. Boo was definitely "in season." I was elated.

Mom had been right. A watched pot never comes "in season."

The first shock of discovery was followed by acute anxiety. I needed a suitable male for the about-to-be-defrocked virgin.

After dinner it was time for a consultation with my ex-assistant groomer and still husband.

"Put the paper down," I said. "I've got something to tell you."

"She's not getting a new front tire until she quits jumping curbs," he said.

"Boo is in season."

"I don't care what she promised."

"Put the paper down and listen. Boo is in season," I yelled.

"That's nice."

"Put down the paper. I want to see your face."

His eyes appeared over the rim of the sports section.

"We have to find her a mate," I told him solemnly.

It finally sunk in.

We had at the outside ten to fourteen days to find a well-bred mate, discuss the suitability of the match, scratch together the not-so-small sum of money for a stud fee, and consummate the act. None of this would guarantee a box full of bouncing puppies. You breed them and then chew your fingernails for sixty-three days. With her track record, I was in for a lot of nail chewing.

We found our virgin queen a consort with two days to spare. She thoroughly enjoyed her 125-mile ride, sitting in solitary splendor on the back seat chewing on her endless supply of chewy cookies. On arrival she descended regally from her carriage and was introduced to her waiting swain, who nearly swooned at the first inviting sniff. He touched her back with one tentative paw, and she turned into a raging hag, threatening to

behead or disembowel him before his owner managed to rescue the bewildered amour.

It was embarrassing.

"What's the matter with you?" I bellowed.

There was another approach, another snarl, and another attempted decapitation. The male was skulking around behind his owner's legs. He looked discouraged.

"I think he's going down," his equally discouraged-looking owner observed. King Kong would have gone down under her assaults.

I hauled my reluctant virgin over to the far side of the yard for a heart to heart.

"Listen you. You've got a choice. My foot or his you know what. I'm tired of your nonsense. Now we're going back over there, you're going to act like a lady, and when it's over you can have a whole box of chewy cookies on the way home." She was such a glutton, I hoped bribery would work.

Very firmly I marched her back over to the marriage couch where the male's owner was still looking dubious. He did coax her swain, by now slightly the worse for wear and tear, back to the arena, and we were ready to "have another go at it," as the British say.

She tricked him. The poor devil got within an ace of victory when she turned on him and practically mopped up the yard with him. She did everything except toss him over her head like an enraged bull. The only thing worse than a woman scorned is a really determined virgin.

By now the stud dog's owner was having a fit.

"Oh my God!" he was yelling. "I've never seen one this bad in over thirty years in dogs." He made it clear to us that he wasn't willing to risk his stud dog on another go at it.

Boo finally lost her virginity in the unromantic atmosphere of the veterinarian's office.

On the ride home she sulked, ignored her chewies, and nursed her damaged ego.

The financer of the forced nuptials nursed a damaged bank account as he drove the 125 miles back home to Sherwood Meadows. The unexpected visit to the vet's office on a Sunday added another twenty dollars to Boo's already sizable dowry.

I rode with dreams and counted the days. In sixty-three days we'd better have a whelping box full of bouncing baby Boos or she'd be sorry.

7

Preparations for the "lying in" were in full swing. From the garage the sounds of the nightly carpentry sessions were reassuring. Something called a whelping box was taking shape out there, amidst a lot of sawing, hammering, and profanity.

WHANG! that's the sound of the hammer being thrown on the cement floor.

BOOM! that's the sound of the back door being flung open and kicked shut.

STOMP! STOMP! STOMP! that's the carpenter crossing the kitchen floor.

"#*##*! hammer, **#*##*! box. Wouldja look at my finger?"

"Did you hit it again?"

"You're **#***# right, I hit it again. Is it bleeding?"

"No, but it looks a little dark."

"That's because it's too ***#* cold out there to bleed. My blood congeals."

He did look half frozen. I tried to console him with hot coffee. The hot cup brought his injured finger to life and he groaned.

He'd been against the project from the start. We'd had some difference of opinion about what was needed for a successful "lying in." When I had presented him with Plan "A," an all-purpose whelping box for a medium-sized dog, his reaction was negative.

"Why don't we just run her over to St. John's maternity ward and get her a suite?" he'd suggested snidely. He failed to see that for a proper couching she needed a four-by-six-foot carpeted apartment with sliding sides and a fold-back roof.

"Why can't we just get a big cardboard box at the grocery?" he wanted to know.

26

"Because the book says they chew cardboard and it's dangerous."

"She won't chew wood?" he said, gazing at the well-chewed cabinet door bottoms and chair rungs that looked like toothpicks.

"Not her. The puppies."

"Then you'd better start praying they don't take after their mother. She was a sawdust machine until you started keeping her mouth glued shut with chewy cookies," he said.

"Are you warmed up now?" I was anxious to hustle him back to the job before he got too comfortable.

"I'll never be warm again, but I might as well finish the #*## thing." He moped his way back to the garage for another go around with the Plan "A" all-purpose whelping box.

One thing worried me about the project. How were we going to get it into the house once it was finished?

By now every split-level in the Sherwood Meadows subdivision knew something was happening at 722 Tilbury Walk. The word had spread, thanks to younger daughter, the town crier. It wasn't that I minded the news getting around, it was her choice of words that was disturbing.

"My mother's gonna have puppies," was her joyous proclamation. This was leading to a lot of curiosity among the neighbors about what was going on under my car coat. And a few raised eyebrows among the more conservative, who didn't approve of what sounded like a freaky approach to sex education at 722 Tilbury Walk.

"Quit telling people I'm going to have puppies," I admonished.

Half of Sherwood Meadows couldn't wait to see, and the other half wouldn't let their kids play with ours.

We were seeing a lot of our vet again.

By this time I was really into books. One said, "An examination by a licensed veterinarian on the twenty-sixth day will disclose small walnut-sized lumps in the area of the uterine horns. Palpation of the area will indicate the presence of whelps."

We were in the vet's parking lot when he arrived, six minutes late, on the morning of the twenty-sixth day. He was still groggy from a two-in-the-morning case of "We can't find Tippy's rubber ball with the bell in it. We think he might have swallowed it." He played for time with cups of coffee and dull conversation about last night's hockey game. I was chomping at the bit to get started.

I advanced my newly acquired book learning to the finished product of seven years of medical study and four years of private practice. He took a jaundiced view of my medical expertise.

"It doesn't always work," he said, "because for one thing, not all embryos develop the same. And some dogs are too fat to palpate." The last was a direct shot at Boo, sitting at his feet munching on her chewy cookies. He continued, "And most people don't know when conception took place."

"You can eliminate that," I snapped. "I can tell you the exact week, day, hour, and moment it happened."

"You into horoscopes?" he asked.

"Wouldja just look at her, please?" I said tartly.

Boo accepted the indignity of being probed and squeezed with her normal glum disapproval. Between squeezes from him and a steady handout of chewies from me, she grunted her way through the exam.

"Can't feel a thing," was the appalling news.

"There has to be something," I yelled half hysterically. "Do it again. You missed them."

"I already did it twice. I told you that it doesn't always work," he said.

"Then what's that lump back there?" I asked, pointing to a place at the end of her loin that was bulging.

"That's a fat pad over her kidney on that side," he said smugly. Proving that he read books, too.

"This is Monday," I said, "I'll bring her back on Wednesday."

"Won't do any good," he said.

"Well, can't you at least try?" I muttered.

"You can come every day if you want to. It won't make any difference if she isn't in whelp."

As we slouched our way dejectedly toward the door, he sent one final barb: "You'd better cut her back on those chewy cookies. She's too fat."

"What difference does it make?" I flung back. "You just said nothing's going to happen."

28

Boo was watching "Mister Rogers' Neighborhood" on the tube, and I was curled up in an apathetic ball on the couch.

The door banged open.

"How'd things go at the vet's today?" he asked.

"She's gonna have twelve," I lied.

"Oh my God!" he exclaimed, "Is that normal, or is she some kind of an overachiever?"

"The book says hounds have big litters."

He eyed Boo speculatively. "Stand up Boo," he ordered. "Let's take a look at you."

Boo raised herself three inches off of the carpet in a half slump, held it for two seconds, and then slumped back down.

"She doesn't look like she's got twelve of anything in there, except chewies," he said dubiously.

He disappeared into the kitchen with Boo following along behind, hoping for a predinner handout. They came back together, and he leaned against the door frame with a Budweiser in his uninjured hand.

"I'm not building an annex on that whelping box," he declared.

I switched over to a "Lost in Space" rerun and headed for the kitchen to start dinner. Behind me I could hear him warning her: "You better get off your duff and get some exercise, and you'd better cut down on those chewies if you're going to have twelve kids."

And you'd better have something in exactly thirty-seven more days, I told myself, or both of us are going to be out in the garage sitting in your whelping box.

8

By the end of the sixth week, the vet and I agreed. Finally. Boo would have approximately six or seven or eight puppies. Unless she was carrying some up so high he couldn't feel them.

Everything was progressing swimmingly. It was warm enough to take my car coat off and disappoint the neighbors. On our daily prenatal strolls, Boo's condition was obvious enough that our kids were acceptable in polite society again. And I was making a definite effort to taper off her chewies.

The whelping box tilted sideways and with one side temporarily removed, had entered the house by means of a door removal that had precipitated another discussion on the need for such posh surroundings. Boo sniffed it once and then completely disdained any further contact with it.

"She'll love it once the puppies are here," I consoled a pretty put-out carpenter.

"She'd better," he said, nursing his still-darkened and slightly flattened fingers.

Around the end of the seventh week, the ex-carpenter came up with a suggestion.

"Do you think we could manage to have the Slatterys and the Clarkes for dinner and bridge before we close down for the queen's couching?"

"When did you have in mind?" I asked.

"How about the twenty-sixth?"

"That's cutting it pretty close. She's due on the twenty-ninth."

"Well, then, when do you plan to reopen?" he wanted to know.

I thought about Al Clarke, who hated dogs, cats, gerbils,

long-haired Chinese guinea pigs, children under eighteen years of age, and the smoking section on airplanes.

"Probably never for the Clarkes," I said. "He'll never come back when he finds out there have been puppies in the house." Everytime he'd come to our place since Boo arrived, he'd been miserable. He was convinced she was carrying every disease the Atlanta Communicable Diseases Center was about to declare a nationwide alert on. Boo punished him by fawning over him and licking him like a popsicle every time he stood still. She ignored everyone else who came into the house except family members.

"Make it the twenty-sixth, and we'll get it over with," I said.

"Okay, I'll call them in the morning."

I made a black circle on the twenty-sixth, three days before the big red circle on the twenty-ninth.

Boo would be delighted to see her old friend one more time before he outlawed her forever.

9

Boo detested dinner parties.

She hated the vacuum that swept up the yards and yards of hair she'd spent hours scratching off herself and then spreading in a layer over the carpet. She hated the turned-over-to-the-clean-side sofa cushions because she couldn't find her mashed-down spots. She hated the freshly waxed kitchen floor because her well-rounded rump kept sliding out from under during her refrigerator vigils.

Most of all, she hated being made to wait for leftovers until the company was safely out of the way. She didn't understand why some people were upset about dogs licking plates. She especially detested Nancy Neats, who insisted on clearing the table and putting the dishes straight into the dishwasher before Boo had a chance to polish them.

On the evening of the twenty-sixth, Boo threw herself at Al Clarke with her usual effusiveness. He cringed and wrapped himself into a ball on the couch. She flopped across his feet, still watching him adoringly.

"That's the fattest dog I've ever seen in my life," he commented, trying to untangle himself from her embrace.

"She's expecting," I said, concealing my glee at his discomfiture.

"Expecting? What?" he asked nervously.

"Nothing *you* can catch," I said nastily.

"Let's everybody have a drink," husband interrupted, before things got out of hand.

I noticed Al wiping the rim of his glass before he drank.

I should have suspected something when Boo abandoned her favorite nighttime program and disappeared into the breakfast room where the obstetrics ward had been set up.

I was returning the soup bowls to the kitchen when I heard the first sounds.

"It couldn't be! She wouldn't!" I dumped the bowls in the sink and leaned on the counter, listening.

There is only one sound in the world like a newborn puppy's first cry. It's scary, it's thrilling, it's beautiful. It's a new life. Another renewal.

I tore into the breakfast room. There was my beautiful, arrogant, wonderful Beaucoup nursing her firstborn. She glanced up at me from under her wrinkled brow with those soft brown eyes as if to say, "What's all the fuss about?"

"You monster, I love you," I whispered to her.

I hustled the salads into the dining room and set a new record for devouring avocado and grapefruit wedges. I tried to wigwag the news to the builder that the whelping box was a success. He missed my signals.

Everything was becoming a blur. I snatched the salad bowls, finished or not, and made a beeline for the nursery. There were two furry blobs, now. Clean, warm, fed, and sleeping in the corner of the box. Boo was resting between her efforts. I couldn't believe her coolness. I was working on a nervous breakdown.

The carpenter finally caught my signals and came into the kitchen.

"Look in the box," I beamed.

He peeked around the corner.

"Oh my God! . . . But today's the twenty-sixth."

"She didn't read the book," I excused her.

He was impressed, it was plain to see, as he bent over for a closer look and gently touched one small, sleepy head.

"You stay here with her, and I'll serve," he offered.

"Don't worry, she's taking care of everything beautifully," I bragged for my girl. "I'll keep an eye on her just in case she needs us."

"My box is working perfect," he bragged for his share of the event.

Boo looked at both of us. She knew who deserved the credit.

Between the roast beef and the chocolate mousse, puppies three and four arrived. Boo rested through the after-dinner drinks. Luckily neither Nan Slattery nor Connie Clarke was Nancy Neats. The nursery was safe as we moved from the dining room to the living room.

Between the first and the second rubbers of bridge, puppy five arrived. I reneged three times, and Al Clarke glared at me. I ran up his bids and then dumped him and became a semipermanent dummy.

Between the last rubber and the night cap, puppies six and seven debuted, and Boo closed down the show.

I heard Al Clarke remarking to Connie as they walked toward their car, "She's a pretty decent cook, but she's a rotten bridge player."

I felt sorry for Al Clarke and his antiseptic world.

We hung over the whelping box like two kids under a Christmas tree.

"Fantastic!" the carpenter crowed.

"Isn't she spectacular?" I gloated.

"Think we ought to wake the kids?" he asked.

"No," I answered, "She's had a long night. Let her have her babies to herself tonight."

I can't remember how long I sat on the floor next to the box, just watching.

"I'll buy you a thousand chewy cookies tomorrow," I promised in a whisper. But Boo was sound asleep.

I crawled into bed and stretched contentedly.

"By the way," he murmured sleepily from his side of the bed. "Al Clarke wanted to know if you were going to the grocery store between courses tonight."

"Tell Al Clarke to . . . Oh, never mind, he'll never see newborn puppies, poor boob," I said and then fell asleep.

10

As mother dogs go, Boo was absolutely the best one I ever had. A model of efficiency, she set up rules right from the start.

Everyone ate when the cafeteria was open. If any of them tried to sleep through and catch a snack later, she shoved it awake and hustled it up to a faucet. When squabbles broke out over the choicer rear faucets, both contenders were rolled around a couple of times until they came to their senses. She was in charge, and everyone knew it. She was also a spotless housekeeper. The puppies were like shiny new pennies. The box was as clean as a whistle, except for a few spills now and then. Her system worked. They were all fat, healthy, and growing like weeds in a garden. I could never pass the box without bending down and just watching the tiny miracles inside it. What is more satisfying than new life? I loved every one of them.

She was also very prompt.

At six weeks plus two days, she closed down her end of the operation. She was back in the living room munching on her chewy cookies and catching up on "Mister Rogers' Neighborhood." She made it very clear it was my turn now.

When the cafeteria decamped, the pups took a vote and decided to go look for it.

The first escapee was a fuzzy Houdini who somehow figured out that one side of the box was lower than the others. The sight of one of their number free sent the rest of them into a frenzy. Everybody wanted out. They didn't know what was out there but decided it must be good.

They crawled the sides, they hoisted, they hung suspended over the edge rocking back and forth until they either fell back on their duffs or forward onto their skulls. I kept scooping them up and dumping them back into their box-turned-prison. They whined, they howled, they beat themselves up against the sides of the box. It was incredible the amount of energy they mustered. They piled themselves up and used each other as step ladders. I was sure they were getting together to map out their battle strategy when they thought I wasn't watching. They chinned themselves on the edge of the box until they looked like miniature horse thieves swinging on the gallows. They made horrible plopping sounds when they landed on the kitchen tiles. The littlest one had a doggie fly act that was sensational. She simply walked up the sides of the box. I watched her, dumbfounded, and then let her run around as a reward for her agility. Once they were outside they didn't know what to do with themselves, so they howled because they didn't know what to do with themselves. It was a doggie cuckoo's nest.

Herself wouldn't even deign to come to the kitchen door to see if I was boiling up her kids for dinner.

Did I ever *really* hang over that box and murmur, "Beautiful"?

I tried to fill the void in their lives with food—mainly Pablum and milk. Before the days of specially concocted puppy foods, Pablum was the only resource. At least I knew what to expect after shoving several tons of it between toothless gums when the girls were smaller. As any mother will tell you, Pablum is the world's fastest drying cement. When it dries on high chairs, walls, floors, or children, you have a permanent bond; the floor tiles will come up before the Pablum unsticks. Pablum was the forerunner of Krazy Glue. I can't swear to it, but I have a spot on my left forearm that is either a white mole or some leftover Pablum.

They ate five times a day, and five times a day the kitchen turned into a cement factory. As fast as I put the pan on the floor, they raced into it, over it, around it. They took to rolling one another in it. It was a game and they enjoyed it. They lined up like small vampires, watching while I smushed it together. Then one of them blew the bugle, and they charged the pan in a scene of bedlam that left the slightly wounded lying about in bewildered shock. I never quite figured out how they were getting it—through their mouths or through their skin. I had to keep them moving constantly lest they stick to the floor before I could clean them up. The place was taking on the appearance of a Washeteria, with all the towels and cloths I was using to scrub the Pablum off my sticky lovelies. I barely had them cleaned up from one session than it was starting time for the next battle charge. Everyone was having fun except me. I still had a family that still expected three meals a day minimum. I was running an around-the-clock beanery.

Something else was happening—the place was developing a definite odor problem. As if I couldn't smell, my family offered daily reminders.

"Mom, this place smells yukky!"

"So did you before you were housebroken," I said defensively.

At five o'clock the breadwinner opened the front door, reeled back, and then gathering strength plunged through to the kitchen. He also had a suggestion.

"Hon, go out the front door, take a deep breath, and then come back in. See what happens."

"Look, I know what happens. It smells like a hen house in July."

"Could you maybe do something about it?" he pleaded as he flipped the Budweiser tab in the trash can.

What more could I do? At five-minute intervals I was swabbing down the kitchen floor with Clorox and water or picking up small deposits of recycled Pablum. I was up to five gallons of Clorox and seven rolls of paper towels per week, and the amount was rising. It was averaging nearly a roll of towels and a gallon of Clorox per puppy. We were having macaroni casseroles again. Every time I passed the mop, my hand automatically reached out and grabbed it. I'd had to bring it back to the house three times when I'd tried to open my car door and found I still had the mop in my hand. In three months I had mopped my way around the world twice.

"What we need," I said, "is a small fenced-in area outside where they can play."

He flipped another tab into the trash can.

"It's against the subdivision rules to fence in your place," the retired carpenter said, looking down at his nearly healed fingers.

"They won't say anything if we just put up a little playpen for puppies," I encouraged him.

"Wanna bet?"

"You're the big nonconformist who won't enter Sherwood Meadows' Christmas lighting contest," I goaded.

The fence went up with slightly fewer injuries and slightly less profanity. His proficiency was increasing with practice.

They hated it, every soft, fragrant, grassy inch of it. They were developing terrible walking habits—when they walked, which wasn't very often. Mostly they just stood stock still, whining. When they were forced to move, they walked around like there was shattered glass underfoot. They were developing gaits like Tennessee Walkers, high in the front and choppy in the back. Anything to keep their delicate underpinnings from contact with the hated grass.

Their steady howling to be brought back in was nerve-wracking. One week of the racket and I gave in. For appearances' sake, their outside play periods were ten minutes in the morning, or until the pen's builder pulled out of the driveway, and ten minutes in the late afternoon, when the pen builder's car was due back in the driveway.

In between times they rocketed through the house, and I rocketed behind them spraying wildly with Verbena, Spring Mint, and Frangipani. I burned incense for a short time but stopped when the head of the house complained the place smelled like a Chinese house of the dead. Weekends were my worst fear. I prayed, and for the first time in the history of the weather bureau's records, it rained six weekends in a row. Of course, no one expected me to throw the poor babies out in a downpour.

"My God," he lamented. "I've never seen it rain so many weekends in a row."

"Terrible, isn't it?" I rejoiced and burned a few more of the bayberry candles left over from Christmas.

11

The pups inherited their mother's taste for television. Every evening they settled down in splotchy piles in front of the TV munching on their small-bit chewies. Occasionally, squabbles broke out when somebody snatched a chewy off somebody else's pile, but mostly they were glued to the set. They watched the goings on at the U.N. Security Council sessions with the same avid interest they devoted to the "Adventures of Lassie." It was weird. Nobody I talked to had ever heard of dogs so taken with television. But at least it kept them quiet and clean.

They were housebroken by television. The minute a program ended, I jumped up, poked the pile into action, and yelled, "Okay! everybody up. Let's go."

We raced for the door with me in the lead. They threw themselves down the steps, everybody squatted (the boys weren't ready for the big time three-legged act yet), and then we all raced back into the house just in time to see some obnoxious kid telling his mother, "Look, mom, only two cavities."

Another shock was coming.

The pups were close to their four-month anniversary and fall was in the air when the blow fell.

He looked up from his newspaper and said, "Have you picked the one you're going to keep?"

I'd almost forgotten why we'd had the puppies in the first place.

"Not really," I hedged, while my heart did flip-flops.

"Well, you'd better get started," he said.

"I kinda think we'd better hang onto the first best and the second best, just in case."

"In case of what?" he shot back. "That's three dogs. Are you planning on starting a kennel?"

That was sort of in the back of my mind, but now wasn't the time to drop my plan on the family. Not with the lingering scent of eau de puppy still in the house.

"I'll try to pick one this week, and then we'll sell the rest."

I had a lump in my throat as I watched the pile of chubby rumps and the bright puppy eyes that were just beginning to assume the gravity they would hold in maturity. I truly didn't want to sell any of them. I didn't think I could do it. I looked away as tears welled in my eyes.

The subject came up again later in the week.

"Have you picked one yet?" he asked, sounding more insistent.

"I don't know if I can."

"You can't tell, or you can't sell. Which is it?"

The tears started falling. Forgotten was the Pablum and the puddles, the howling and the thousand times I'd stooped and pulled somebody from behind the refrigerator before they'd learned they had a reverse gear. Maybe somebody else wouldn't feel that way, but to me the smell of puppies wasn't the worst thing that could happen to a house.

"I can't sell them," I wailed.

Fortunately one of us had good sense.

"If you really love them," he said, "then you'll do what is best for them. Not what is easiest for you. Every dog deserves its own place in the world. It needs its own family and all the love that family will give it. Because if you are going to be a breeder, then you have to learn; that's what it is really all about."

The final decision was to keep one male and one female. I picked the best male and I cried. He looked like a future star already, with the lovely layback of shoulders and firmness in the rear end that promised he would gait like a smoothly moving machine. From his mother, Boo, he had inherited those same soft brown eyes that would forever stare straight into the hearts of everyone who ever saw him.

I picked the best female and I cried. After a rather longish discussion about increasing the population to three dogs in a subdivision that was already suspicious of us, I selected the bitch I hoped would be good enough to show, but if that wasn't in the cards, then she would become the future foundation bitch of my breeding program. Of course I didn't mention this grandiose plan too explicitly.

I lay for a long time that night staring at the ceiling and wondering. Did I really want to be a breeder? Did I want to face another time and then another time giving up those small lives that had become such a part of mine so quickly? I began to understand all the things behind those words I'd uttered so rashly, "I'll breed one of my own."

The ad went in the Sunday paper and I cried. "BASSET HOUND PUPPIES. AKC-registered. Champion sired. 2 males, 3 females. Tricolor. GOOD HOMES ONLY."

My head said he was right. My heart was broken.

T hings got off to an early start Sunday morning. The first phone call came through at seven-thirty. I slithered an arm out from under the covers, grabbed the receiver, and managed to say hello.

"Are you the party advertising Basset Hound puppies?" a voice inquired.

"Uh huh," I mumbled back.

"How much are you asking for them?" it wanted to know. It didn't know, but it had just disqualified itself. Anybody who asked the price that quickly was a comparison shopper and a dubious candidate for the required "GOOD HOMES ONLY." I quoted a price that knocked its head off. It got even with me.

"Lady, I don't want to buy your whole litter," it barked, and then hung up on me.

"You wouldn't get one if you brought Fort Knox," I barked back at the dead phone.

I staggered toward the kitchen, pausing to flip on the TV for the waiting audience. Through half-open eyes I surveyed them as they sat watching "Bible Stories Brought to Life." They did look spiffy sitting there all bathed and brushed and munching on their breakfast chewies. You could just bet your bippy that anybody who asked the price first wasn't going to get one of those angels.

The phone was ringing like Civil Defense headquarters on a red alert. It rang and rang and rang. The calls were developing a predictable pattern.

"Hello, are you the party advertising Basset Hound puppies?"

"Yes."

The second most popular question after price was age.

42

"How old are your puppies?"

Buyers seemed to have some misguided notion that price is contingent on age. The older the cheaper. Like yesterday's produce at the grocery store.

"Four months."

"Four months! Isn't that awfully old? Are you having trouble getting rid of them?"

I restrained myself from crawling through the phone. Instead, I patiently explained that, no, four months is not old. I just did not choose to sell them sooner. I thought about my babies watching "Bible Stories" and decided. This one was going to get the business, too. She was already convinced that something must be wrong with them. She would always be convinced she'd bought something that was second-choice merchandise. I quoted her a hair-raising price, and she faded away.

In between the age- and price-checkers, I was listening to a whale of a lot of old wives' tales. Apparently quite a few people didn't have much to do with themselves on Sunday mornings. Did I know, they would ask, that females were better watch dogs than males?

I had to admit that I didn't know that.

"Because females don't bum, and males do," they told me smugly. I don't know if anyone has ever conducted a poll to see how many strays are male versus female, but given the chance every dog capable of putting one foot in front of the other will bum sometime. Sex doesn't have a thing to do with it.

I was also told by other experts that "spaded" (their word for "spayed") females always wind up fat. I never convinced a one of them when I explained that the surgery didn't have a thing to do with it. Any dog who doesn't exercise and who overeats gets obese. Sexual appetite or lack of it doesn't have a thing to do with it.

The best one I heard was the elderly gentleman who asked me quite seriously if they had been given their weekly garlic ration.

"What on earth would I give them garlic for?" I asked, perplexed.

"Only way to get rid of them worms, lady," he said, very assured.

"They most certainly have not been given garlic," I growled back at him for even suggesting I'd give them such a thing.

"Must have a mighty wormy bunch of pups," he said and

hung up before I could get back at him.

For the ones who passed the telephone screening, I began setting up appointments. A couple of the pups got bored with "Face the Nation" and wandered into the kitchen. I couldn't look them in the eye. I started to lose my nerve. I was hatching a plot to keep all of them when I was jolted back to reality.

"What time will the first ones be here?" he asked.

"One o'clock," I said.

"Good. We can eat lunch, and I'll take the kids to the matinee so they don't see the puppies leaving."

"I wish I were dead," I moaned.

"You'll get over it," he philosophized.

The second shock of the day came when the first prospects showed up and the old philosopher turned into an instant St. Francis of Assisi. After he'd chased off the first three prospects, I began to wonder if anybody would meet his standards.

The first one got chased while we were standing around talking and their little Eddie tried to dislocate one of the pup's front legs.

"Put the puppy down, sonny," St. Francis said through gritted teeth.

Little Eddie promptly dropped the pup kerplunk on the floor.

"Sorry, folks," he said, "I don't think your kid's ready for a dog yet." He held the door open for them, glaring, with two hundred pounds of persuasion, just in case they wanted to argue. Little Eddie's screams could still be heard as the car turned off Tilbury Walk onto the main street.

"Wouldja believe some people?" he grunted disgustedly.

The next couple suffered a similar fate for a different reason. Under cross-examination they revealed that the railroad tracks were about a hundred feet from their backyard.

"Is your yard fenced?" St. Francis asked so quietly I knew they were doomed.

"No," the man admitted, "but that won't be a problem. I'm gonna train the dog not to go near the railroad tracks."

They didn't even get to see the pups. They were very angry as they stomped down the walk.

I was getting the idea that St. Francis was going to be a tough nut to crack.

Then the tide turned and the wonderful ones began coming.

The first was a family almost like our own. Their eyes and

their faces told the story. The children handled the pups gently and with experience. All the puppies loved them. We couldn't find a single reason to turn them down. I handed them a bag of puppy meal and a farewell sack of chewies. I hugged my girl for a final time and waved goodbye as she rode off snuggled in the children's arms. And I cried.

Another of the girls went with a middle-aged couple I knew would spoil her rotten. And they did. She ate with them, slept with them, traveled with them, and when it rained and they had to take her for her walks, they shielded her with an umbrella. She was always too fat when she returned for family reunions.

The last of the three little girls went with a young couple who wanted her badly but couldn't afford the price we asked.

"Please, if we give you what we have, can we pay the rest each week?" they pleaded.

They were so young and wanted her so very much.

"Don't worry that we won't take care of her," they promised. "She'll eat the same as us." I knew that she would.

We looked at the couple—the boy in his outgrown high school letter sweater and often-washed chinos, his wife with the fresh scrubbed look of barely-beyond-the-teens, shyly twisting the new gold band on her finger. They gave us their slender hoard, and we handed half of it back to them and told them untruthfully it was a discount because she was the biggest eater. The glow lasted long after they disappeared around the end of the street.

Every Christmas until she went to sleep at fourteen, we got a card and a picture of Angelina under the Christmas tree.

We made one mistake—but they did seem nice. They were looking for a male. Yes, we still had two males. I described one. He was the right color, size, age, and shape, exactly what they were dying for. When they arrived they told us they had no children, but a large house and a fenced yard. And oh, yes, they assured us, they had had dogs before. My mistake was in not asking how many dogs and what had happened to them. Perhaps I was taken in by a Calvin Klein pantsuit and a Coupe de Ville in my driveway. Later I would learn not to be a snob. Maybe if I had just noticed how little they touched him. Maybe I wanted to believe too badly.

I packed his belongings, the bag of puppy meal, the sack of chewies, hugged him, and cried again.

Through my tears I didn't see them carefully draping the back seat with oil cloth before they plopped him down untouched in solitude. He left with no one's arms around him. St. Francis saw and winced but said nothing to me. I think he guessed what was coming.

Stanley bombed. He was the last of the males that were up for adoption. I hated the cold sound of up for sale, so I called it up for adoption.

A few more people came, and either we didn't like them or they didn't like Stanley. We gave up and decided we would advertise Stanley as a singleton next Sunday. I was secretly glad I would have him around for another week.

The living room seemed strangely empty. Boo and the survivors watched TV and munched quietly on their chewies.

The kids were subdued. St. Francis looked worried. He still didn't like the couple in the Coupe de Ville. I sniffled and sniffled and sniffled.

We were all shaken by the day's events. I had a hunch that Stanley's ad would never go in the Sunday paper. What was one more dog if you already have three?

I would find that out when the Coupe de Ville couple sent Stanley's brother back home to roost.

13

Exactly five days after I'd packed his belongings and he'd left us, Stanley's brother was back. He brought with him a sack of almost untouched chewies. The chewies were one of her list of complaints, as she told me over the phone. "His chewies made his breath smell odd, and his stool had a tinge of yeasty odor." I could imagine the look on her face as she was describing the results of his chewy habit.

I guess I'd been living with clouds of chewy breath for so long I'd never noticed.

I checked the list of ingredients on the box. Sure enough it said "traces of brewer's yeast."

But that wasn't the main complaint against him. He had a list of failings as long as his body. They began at his mouth and worked back to his tail. Besides the previously mentioned halitosis, he slobbered when he drank water, which he seemed to do constantly. Her kitchen carpeting was looking very seedy now. He also shed, whined, scratched himself (making thumping sounds), dumped his food pan, and didn't respond too promptly when called. These were minor complaints. The big one she saved for last. He'd had two spells of flatulence. Terribly embarrassing. Twice guests were present, and twice he'd lit up the place with a noisy display of expelled gas. At first they hadn't suspected the dog, and it was a bit tense among the guests. Things had improved slightly when they'd pinned the blame on the dog. But all the same, she'd been humiliated.

"Most of those things you've described are natural traits of Basset Hounds," I said, "except for the flatulence. I don't understand that."

"Well, he just won't do." She was very snappish.

"Alright," I snapped back. "Pack his things and bring him back if he doesn't suit you."

"Will there be any charges for the time we've had him?" she inquired.

"Absolutely not," I yelled. "This isn't a Rent-a-Dog Service, you know. Just bring him back."

While I waited for her, I wished that I could just scratch her patronizing face. I'd caught the implication in her question. She thought we sold dogs for a living. If she only knew how fast I'd starve to death if that were true.

The Coupe de Ville was in the driveway in fifteen minutes. Just enough time for me to work up a head of steam if anything were wrong with the dog when he arrived.

Stanley's brother hopped out as soon as the door opened, rushed down the walk toward the door, gave me one hello wag, and zoomed into the living room. He made the rounds, saying his "Hi, gang!" and plopped down in front of the TV for the three o'clock rerun of "Sesame Street." I made him a secret promise. He would never leave again, no matter what. And I named him Walter.

I returned the Calvin Klein pantsuit's money in full.

I had just one question.

"Why," I asked, "did you want the dog in the first place?"

Her answer was the all-time worst reason for wanting a dog I have ever heard.

She told me quite seriously that her husband had just received a big promotion. They had sold their contemporary home and bought a large Colonial home in one of the posher sections of Boltonville. The entire house had been done in authentic Williamsburg by an excellent interior decorator. The Poodle who had been so appropriate for the contemporary house wouldn't do in the new Colonial setting.

They had decided that the new decor needed a hound. A Basset Hound seemed so outdoorsy, so woodsy—a perfect finishing touch.

As she was leaving she told me in her breathy finishing school voice, "We named him Wellington. After the Revolutionary War general."

"His name is Walter," I shot back, "and Wellington fought at Waterloo."

I've always wondered about Walter. He never had another

attack of flatulence in the twelve years that he lived.

I stretched out on the couch after she left and reviewed my story about Walter's return when St. Francis returned home.

He wasn't surprised.

"I didn't think he'd last that long," he said.

14

This morning I had a big surprise for my earlier selection of a future show star, Apollo. (I had finally gotten around to naming him. His name had been chosen because I had some delirious idea that he was just the beginning of a series of winners who would require the whole pantheon of Greek gods for names.) He was watching cartoons on the tube as usual with the rest of his family.

As I cleared away the breakfast things, I dreamed of streamers of blue ribbons and shelves spilling over with glittery silver bowls and trays and butter sets and maybe even, some day, one of those champagne coolers they sometimes gave for Best in Show. I slammed the dishwasher closed just as I was placing the champagne cooler in the glass-fronted trophy case the carpenter would be building, once I started bringing home goodies again.

Before he got too deep into "Captain Kangeroo," I shuffled through the pile, extracted Apollo from underneath Stanley, who was licking chewy dribble off his head, warned Stanley to knock it off before he gave him a bald spot, and headed my future star toward the basement.

He didn't like it. In fact the first three days' training sessions were taken up trying to convince Apollo it was safe to be underground.

"Look out the windows, silly," I kept telling him. "See, we're not in the catacombs."

He wasn't convinced. He kept watching over his shoulder, which led to a lot of bumping into things when we sailed around the basement as I tried to teach him to gait. He never believed *he* bumped into things. Things suddenly sprang up and bumped into him.

He was not an apt pupil. He picked things up very slowly.

After two full weeks of the course, he was still swinging his head wildly every time I slipped the lead around his neck. He behaved like he'd been executed as a horse thief in an earlier life. Every time one of the crew upstairs jumped from the furniture onto the floor, he panicked. He hated thunder.

The basement rang with our squabbling.

"Stop that you dummy, before your head falls off," I'd shout.

Shouting at him made him shake his head more. Insulted at my yelling, he'd bawl and make a break for the stairway. Trapping him was like trying to swat a fly with the telephone book. He just sort of oozed out of my grasp.

We had two major problems with his gaiting—after I caught him, of course. He either flatly refused to budge and didn't care if his head came off when I yanked him with the lead, or once started he was unstoppable. From a dead start, he'd rev up to Mach 2 and we'd go careening around the basement in large circles, small circles, dodging posts, scraping walls, making figure eights around the washing machine until he saw his chance and made a beeline for the stairs and tried to decapitate both of us on the open stair risers. When we'd stop to catch our breath, I'd plead with him.

"Why must you be so hostile? Is it too much to ask of you to just walk around for a few minutes without trying for a murder and suicide?"

He was unimpressed. He knew I couldn't prove a thing.

It's hard to describe our attempts at posing him. The word that comes to mind is acute slumping. By him. I was getting close to hating him. As long as I held his head and his tail and kept one knee in about his center portion, he stayed upright. The moment I released him, he splattered down like an overturned bowl of gelatin.

I was convinced it had to be some sort of exotic muscle disorder. No dog could be that treacly. Unless he were the most outrageously contrary dog on earth. I gave him the benefit of the doubt.

We cancelled one session and went to the vet's instead.

"Wouldja take a look at him?" I said. "I think he's got some sort of muscle disorder."

"Why? What's he doing?" he asked.

"He can't stand up unaided," I said.

"What's he doing now?" he inquired.

He had his eye on the dummy, who was standing at a "present arms" that would have won first prize in a U.S. Marine Corps drill.

I resisted pounding him into a puddle on the spot. He was doing it to embarrass me.

"He won't do it at home. He's only doing it now to show off," I said accusingly.

"If he can do it once, he can do it again," he said, sounding very assured.

"Then you think he's okay?"

"You're fine, aren't you, fella," he said, punching him playfully in the ribs. He promptly dissolved into a jellylike mass on the examining table.

"See what I mean?" I crowed victoriously.

The jellylike mass promptly rose to its feet and stood at attention.

"See what I mean?" the vet said patronizingly.

I was furious at both of them.

"Give him a shot," I ordered.

"For what?"

"For being a miserable, hard-headed, stupid dog."

He shook his head at both of us and put stupid's card back in the file.

We shuffled out of the office together. I tried to act like we weren't together, which wasn't easy since he kept making figure eights between my legs.

"Now you can't even walk," I grumbled at him.

We had a talk on the way home in the car, or at least I talked. He was busy hanging over the back seat watching the cars behind us.

"Alright, you," I said. "That was a great performance in there, but don't forget I'm the party you live with. You have a pretty short memory about where your chewies come from. I'm telling you now for the last time. You either learn to stand up, or you've seen your last 'Sesame Street' for a month. I mean it."

I wished he'd quit smiling and egging on the drivers behind us. They kept inching closer to see what that funny-looking thing was in the back of the car. One of these days I was going to get one of those cute little stickers that said, "DON'T TAILGATE. SHOW DOGS."

Just as soon as I had a show dog.

15

Nobody is perfect. Apollo and I were proof of that statement.

In spite of our less-than-polished performance, I decided we were ready to make our debut at the dog shows. I based my decision on the fact that we weren't running into as many things, my elbows were almost healed from where I'd ricocheted off the basement walls, and I'd worked out a system that wasn't too noticeable for keeping him from slumping when we posed. I'd discovered that pinching him had a sudden electrifying effect that lasted long enough for me to scratch my nose or smooth my skirt underneath me when I squatted. I was optimistic. He wasn't. His cooperative days were still outnumbered by his uncooperative ones. I kept part of my promise about "Sesame Street." For every Mach 2 getaway, he missed seeing Big Bird. It was partly successful.

I picked the Sunday after Thanksgiving for our debut and broke the news to him while he could still smell the turkey hash.

"Listen, big shot, you want to go bye-bye with me?" I asked. The only bye-bye he knew was going to the vet's, and he was puzzled about why he was being asked. He'd never been consulted before. It made him suspicious.

"Not to the vet's, dummy," I hastened to reassure him. "Far, far away. Just you and me." I tried building it up. "And you'll meet all kinds of new friends."

He was apathetic.

"Well you're going whether you like it or not," I said.

If he was apathetic about his upcoming bye-bye, he wasn't apathetic about the Saturday night ceremonial that preceded it.

For someone who had never had a full bath before, he was

very certain he wouldn't like it. Why, I don't know. He was totally opposed to immersion in water. He went down in final defeat under a hail of determined humans hauling different sections of him to the tin tub in the basement. His last bit of resistance collapsed when his paws became waterlogged.

While he stood watching morosely, I tried to make a decision from the breathtaking array of dog shampoos I had accumulated during Boo's short career. Dog shampoos tend to proliferate like untended gerbils. There are shampoos for black dogs, white dogs, tan dogs, yellow dogs, and wild boar dogs. Dogs with long coats, short coats, dry skin, oily skin, and skins with galloping eczema. Not to mention a certain shampoo that practically guaranteed a champion in every bottle. Arrayed against these magic workers were the old standbys: Castile soap for purity, cocoa butter soap for dogs with fly-away coats, and Joy. It makes dogs squeaky clean, just like dishes.

Apollo waited while I picked and poked among the shampoos for just the right one to bring out his beauty. We had a problem. He didn't exactly fit any of the shampoos. His coat was a mélange of black, white, and tan. To color-treat him properly, I decided on a combination of black, tan, and white shampoos. Hopefully, each would work on the proper color.

As it turned out, they didn't. His colors blurred. The white was tattletale gray, he got ring around the color from the black shampoo, and his tan turned to mud. He looked pretty seedy standing there in his tin tub with the rinse water dripping off him. I knew what had to be done, but I didn't relish it.

He was something less than gleeful when he was dropped back into the tub for a second go-around. I doused him with Joy until he was restored to his normal scheme. Two baths in rapid succession had stripped his natural oils and left him with a fly-away coat. I debated and then decided against any further maneuvers. Better he went in the morning looking like an aroused porcupine.

I led him back upstairs still slightly shaken from two baths and sent him to my bedroom to avoid contact with the rest of the unwashed mass, who were attempting self-immolation around the fireplace.

While Apollo was making damp spots in my bed, fluff-drying himself, I floated to tidyness in a tub of Jean Naté's fresh lemon bubbles.

We sailed out of the driveway before dawn the next morning in a cloud of fresh lemon and squeaky clean. If cleanliness is next to godliness, then we were halfway up Jacob's ladder. We couldn't miss, I told myself as we ramped down onto the Interstate.

He was so sparkly and alert (for him) and lovable riding along checking the highway traffic for me. He couldn't lose. I felt kinda sharp myself in my Pendleton plaid pants and matching Shetland sweater that was going to be my Christmas present. We were a team out for a victory. No judge with an eye in his head could turn us down.

A very tacky looking judge gave us fourth place in a class of four.

We resumed our training sessions. I figured that our margin before the next outing had moved up to about forty percent. As a backup measure, I used up two bottles of the championship-guaranteed shampoo. Neither bottle had a blue ribbon in the bottom.

We were both getting discouraged. I was tired of driving, and he was tired of missing his favorite programs.

We went back to the basement. We changed shampoos again. We might not have been the most polished performers, but we were certainly the most practiced and the cleanest in the shows. It should have counted for something.

After our third defeat, I was beginning to agree with the ringside gossips—the American Kennel Club only licensed people who were partially sighted. We'd managed to meet three half-blind ones in three weekends. Another word cropped up among the losers—politics. I remembered all those choco-marsh cakes. My God, I thought, is it back to that again?

On the way home, I talked it over with Apollo. I tended to agree with his opinion, although it was a bit self-serving, that tidiness was not as important as the books had indicated. Today was a perfect example. The blue ribbon winner had little mud balls between his toes, and his canines were coated with plaque.

"Open your mouth, let's see your choppers," I said.

He grinned, displaying his snowy white canines recently scraped by the vet at the slight charge of $20. I chucked him under the chin, and he rolled over in a fit of camaraderie.

"Watch the chewy dribble," I warned. "These are my Christmas pants."

He rested his snowy paws on my knee as I switched on the car radio, and we rolled home through the darkness.

"How did it go today?" asked my retired assistant groomer.

"It's politics," I answered.

16

After three washouts it was pretty discouraging.
Apollo was shell shocked from three successive total immersions, and I was tired of getting up before dawn and driving to bean patches and county fairgrounds.
The prospects were gloomy. It wasn't going to be easy explaining how I'd accumulated five dogs without a show stopper among them. I could have done the same thing at the city dog pound and gotten a star in my crown for doing a good deed. I needed a victory to put some pizzazz in me and to give some answers for the questions that were going to be asked pretty shortly.

I decided to change dogs to see if it would change my luck.

I went back to the pile in front of the TV and started turning dogs over. I went through the pile twice, just to be sure.

It didn't take much of an eye to tell that the returnee, Walter, was close to hopeless. He looked like he'd been wired together by a drunken crew of angels or fairies or whatever it is that puts baby dogs together in babyland. Nothing fit properly. It all just hung together because it had no place else to go. He was even more gelatinous than Apollo. He was also very phlegmatic. Not too good a recommendation for a career that needed at least some showmanship.

Aphrodite, the girl, wasn't ready. She needed a bit more here and a bit less in different spots. She also needed fewer chewies, I decided, when I noticed she was developing hip pads and a definite droop in her belly region. She was warned.

"Aphrodite, you're spending too much flop time and not enough go time."

I was down to a single choice: Stanley.

He didn't exactly set me on fire, but I needed some kind of answer for the question I knew was coming pretty soon, "How you doing with your show dog?"

I took a deep breath, stretched Stanley out, and nearly gave up. Stanley was a real "hang loose" nonchalant. If I had stood him with one foot wrapped around his head, he would have stayed that way. He was overtrainable.

We went to a crash course of training sessions. What Stanley may have lacked in spirited performance he made up for with his safety-first attitude. He never truly worked up enough interest in the proceedings to cause problems. We shuffled around the basement like two dry-land ice skaters. He mistrusted everything.

"Look, Stanley," I'd appeal to him, "can't you pick more than one foot off the floor at a time? You're *not* going to fall over." We'd shuffle a few more steps, he'd stop and examine his feet to see if he was wearing out his pads, and then we'd move again. He was driving me up the walls.

"Now you listen here, Stanley," I'd bark at him. "Those feet are going to last you for the next fifteen years, so stop checking them every three steps."

He didn't believe me.

At least posing him was easy. It was getting him going again that was unnerving. I thought of running him into the vet's for a narcolepsy check, but considering some of my previous claims of exotic disorders among my dogs, I skipped the vet and began stuffing Stanley full of vitamins. I gave him enough to drive a normal dog straight up the walls. All it did for Stanley was increase his already ravenous appetite. I couldn't afford to feed him and buy that many vitamins, so I gave up the vitamins.

The questioning was getting more pointed. As a matter of fact, they were becoming point-blank demands.

"Did you give up showing dogs?" my husband was inquiring.

Ready or not, I would debut Stanley.

To answer the questions, why had I switched dogs and why had Stanley, a former leftover, been elevated to prime show dog position, I made excuses. Apollo wasn't quite at his peak. I'd decided to hold him back awhile. Sometimes dogs get a poor reputation if they keep losing.

"Is Stanley at his peak?" he asked, bewildered at the sudden shift.

"I won't know until I try him in a few shows," I answered with what I hoped sounded like someone who knew what she was doing.

"Boy, he's a surprise," was the perplexed answer.

"Lots of the top breeders don't always pick the right one the first time," I said airily.

"I don't think I would have picked Stanley the first time myself," he said in a voice that indicated he still wouldn't pick Stanley.

I went ahead anyway. Maybe Stanley would surprise me.

Came our first outing together and Stanley surprised me. He came alive for the first and last time in his life.

Maybe if he had lifted his head just once while we were plodding around the ring he might have been better able to cope, but the way things turned out he was totally unprepared for what happened.

The judge that day was a lady of more than ample proportions who fancied merry widow hats and tent dresses with enormous batwing sleeves.

We'd finished making our desultory stroll around, and Stanley was leaning drowsily against my knee in what was as close to a pose as he ever got, when she swooped in over him like Dracula on the wing. He had absolutely no idea of what was happening when his world suddenly turned into black silk. He jumped twice his own height straight up in the air, hovered for what seemed like seconds, and came down in a perfect three-point landing. It was a near perfect take-off and re-entry. It would have been better if he had just fainted; we would have caused less of a stir. The other dogs were rattling around trying to get under the shaky fence, some had climbed into their surprised owners' arms, a few just squatted down and began moaning. Dogs and people were milling around like someone had just shouted, "Earthquake."

The judge was thoroughly miffed with Stanley. She walked over and marked something in her book and then ignored us for the rest of the time we were in the ring.

I tried to console him on the way home.

"Look, don't let it get you," I said soothingly. "How many times do you think you're going to meet a 747 making a landing with empty tanks at a dog show?"

His attitude was hurting us. After his one moment of liveliness, he reverted to his noncommital stance.

Stanley was a flower child who didn't understand what all the hullabaloo was about. He'd offer his paw to other dogs, and they'd snap at it. The noise and the rushing around wore him out. Most of all, he couldn't understand why he was supposed to keep running around in a circle. As far as he could tell, if you'd seen one ring you'd seen them all.

We tried one last time.

Things were going badly, I could feel it. He was even more listless and dispirited than usual. We barely managed to make it around the ring, and when I posed him, he kept leaning worse and worse. A couple of times he nearly knocked both of us flat on our backsides. I kept shoving him upright; I prodded him, I punched, I swore in his ear. I promised to beat him to a pulp if both of us ever got out of the place. One time he leaned away from me and simply keeled over on his side. Embarrassed, I explained to the people on either side of us he hadn't suffered cardiac arrest, he was just showing off. The judge was a few steps away from us when I tried the last trick I had in my bag. I decided to appeal to his sportsmanship. I didn't think he had any, but there had to be something that would stir him. In a low voice so that the others couldn't hear, I reminded him of his favorite late, late movie. The one with Knute Rockne and the Fighting Irish and the bands playing.

Stanley perked up for a minute, and I thought I had him. I redoubled my efforts. I went for the big locker room scene.

"Come one, Stanley," I spurred him on. "Let's go boy. Let's get one for the Gipper!"

It was instant disaster. His normal glum outlook turned into complete dejection. It was too much for him. I wound up nearly having to carry his limp figure from the ring.

Stanley was never going to peak. Stanley was never going to be ready for the big time. Stanley was born to sit on sunny hillsides and watch the flowers in the valley below.

I returned him to the pile and sat back to think things over. I'd wait for spring and maybe try again.

We settled down to the long winter. Five dogs, two kids, logs in the fireplace, and outside the snow was building up in the puppy playpen.

17

Things were running smoothly except for one thing—I was beginning to worry about Walter.

He didn't seem to be developing any interests. Not that the others were balls of fire, but at least when the doorbell rang they raised their heads. Walter barely disturbed the wrinkles on his forehead.

The best description of Walter was that he had a phlegmatic personality. He reminded me of a kid who didn't throw a screaming fit when he got a set of encyclopedias instead of a bicycle for Christmas. It just wasn't natural to be that dormant.

I brought the subject up a couple of times with not too much success.

"I don't know what's wrong with Walter," I said one afternoon during a football game. "He acts depressed to me."

"Wait until halftime, and we'll talk about it," the ex-fullback put me off.

At halftime he said, "Alright, what's wrong with Walter? Ain't he eating?"

"Of course he's eating. But there's more to dogs than eating."

"Not with this bunch."

"Maybe it comes from that stomach problem he had. Remember when Boo's milk gave him diarrhea, and we had to switch him to Esbilac?"

He remembered.

"He cost more to feed than the kids did," he said.

I wished I hadn't reminded him.

"Why don't you run him into the vet's?"

"And tell him I think I've got a depressed dog?" After the visits for imaginary lumps that turned out to be fat pads and a muscle disorder that was plain laziness, I wasn't going back to tell the vet I thought I had a Section Eight depressive dog.

Halftime was nearly over. I was going to lose his attention when the bands marched off the field.

"Well, get him in here, and let's take a look at him."

"Walter!" I shrilled.

Apollo, Stanley, and Aphrodite all came in.

"Walter!" I shrilled again.

"Maybe he doesn't know his name," he suggested.

"He knows his name," I said. "He just doesn't care enough to come."

I banged into the kitchen where Walter was sitting, waiting for the refrigerator door to open. It was the only thing that interested him. One day while I'd been taking the milk off the top shelf, Walter had lifted a whole head of lettuce from the bottom shelf.

"Walter, get your backside into the living room," I yelled in his ear. He moved sluggishly toward the living room and slouched down in front of the couch. The ex-fullback switched his attention from the "Dixie Darlings" marching off the field to Walter.

"My God!" he exclaimed looking at him.

Walter had to be seen to be appreciated. He was eighty pounds of saggy Basset Hound, with feet like frying pans, eyes that always seemed to be viewing an unspeakable tragedy, and a jelly bean body.

"See what I mean?" I said.

"I see that you'd better cut down on his chewies. He's too fat to care, *that's* his problem." He turned back to the TV for the second-half kickoff.

"Thank you, doctor," I flung at him as I headed the group out to the kitchen. Walter led the others one step behind me.

I tried talking to him when the others weren't around. Maybe he needed more personal attention. Some nights after the others were asleep, I'd curl up in front of the fireplace with Walter and try to boost his lagging spirits.

"Listen, Walter," I'd say, "you're one seventh of a $300 stud fee. You drank five cases of Esbilac, and that stuff isn't cheap. You've had $60 worth of puppy shots and $35 worth of D-H-L shots so you wouldn't get nasty diseases. Add it all up, Walter, it's a pretty hefty sum. And you have a very healthy appetite."

Walter's response indicated he didn't count his worth in

money. I thought maybe he felt left out because he hadn't been invited to the training sessions in the basement. Perhaps it would help if I could prove to him he could do something besides overturn his food pan, which he habitually approached like a bull elephant in the rutting season. Maybe Obedience School would end his constant inward searching and raise his self-esteem. It was worth a try. Walter attended classes under protest, criticizing the curriculum (which I took as a hopeful sign—at least he was somewhat interested), refusing to cooperate, and interfering with the more serious students striving diligently for their Companion Dog diplomas at the course's completion. This wasn't endearing us to the class or to the instructor. Walter spent most of his classtime huddling up against my legs, slobbering great globs of white drool onto my slacks and staring wistfully at the door. He also howled intermittently at being away from home after dark. Walter's disruptions were definitely making us unpopular. We left the classes by mutual consent after the night Walter was finally roused from his lethargy during the sit and stay exercise by all those unguarded tempting rumps around him. He decided to conduct a sexual preference survey among his classmates while their owners were too far away to interfere. Walter's inquisitive nose nudging its way down the line of dogs broke up the exercise. There is no place in Obedience School for anti-establishment types, so we gracefully took our leave.

Secretly I was encouraged by his nonconformist spunk.

Within reason I did allow him to make his own decisions to help build his confidence. However, going to the vet's for shots was not a decision he could be trusted with. He hadn't inherited his mother's affection for the doctor. Shortly after we dropped out of Obedience School, he developed a stomach upset. We spent a long day of smelly diarrhea, and I dosed him with half a bottle of Pepto-Bismol. When that didn't work, I sorted him out of the pile and announced, "Walter, put your chewies away and get yourself together. We have to go bye-bye."

Fortunately, another of Walter's failings was a poor memory. He never remembered the last time he'd gone bye-bye was a trip to the vet's and included a large needle in his fat rump.

Somewhere during his scuffing through last fall's dead leaves on the lot in front of the vet's office, Walter turned up a thoroughly dead pigeon. He wasn't a pretty sight as he carried it over to me with its legs sticking stiffly out of one side of his mouth and its vacant dead eyes staring sightlessly from the other. I started to gag.

When we reached the door, I said, "Walter, put your bird down. You can pick it up on the way out."

Walter stood foursquare like the queen's guards at Buckingham Palace, clutching his new friend.

"Walter, I'm serious. Put that thing down," I said more forcefully.

We stood there eyeball to eyeball.

Then the door opened, and Walter pushed his way past a well-dressed matron cuddling a well-dressed Yorkie into the waiting room.

It was very quiet in the waiting room as we sat down.

"He misses his chewies," I explained sheepishly.

Walter was unabashed at the horrified looks we were drawing as the sickening smell of dessicated pigeon mixed with the ether smells from early morning surgery. The vet looked out of his examining room door, sniffed, and jumped Walter over the rest of the waiting patients. In the examining room, there was none of our usual bantering. I explained his problem, he plunged a giant-sized needle into Walter's rump, gasped, and shoved us out the door.

Outside the office Walter tired of his new friend and dropped it back among the leaves, wagging at me as if he had proved his point. I never figured out his point, God knows, but it satisfied him.

He suffered no aftereffects from his affaire de pigeon. There was barely any improvement in his psyche, and he lapsed back into his lethargic refrigerator watching. All was not quite lost. On subsequent visits to the vet's, he was treated with a respect he'd never received before—lest he find again and drag into the sterile surroundings a larger and more odiferous cadaver.

Through the years I've wondered sometimes if maybe, just maybe, the Walters of the world are put here to prove that even the least of us can leave our mark somewhere, sometime.

18

I was having a lot of sinking spells lately, brought on by questions that caused sudden heart droppings and nervous twitchings.

"Mom, can I tell the kids at school that Stanley and Apollo are champion dogs?"

"NO!"

"Well, you said they were gonna be as soon as they were big enough, huh, mom?" Younger daughter still believes in Santa Claus and the Easter Bunny and that mothers speak the gospel truth.

"Well, they're sure as heck big enough," older daughter interjects her bit. Older daughter has reached the age of cynicism about mother's statements. I try for a snappy comeback, but she's got me, temporarily.

"Well, how much bigger do they have to get, huh, mom?" Younger daughter, besides being a true believer, is also tenacious.

"Daddy says if they get any bigger we're gonna put saddles on them." Older daughter is getting very close to a rap in the teeth.

"Very funny. Where are you and your daddy opening your act? You'll kill 'em in Peoria," I say. Proving that all the wit in the family isn't on one side of the family.

"Well, how big do they have to be before they're champions? Huh, mom?" The kids have also been seeing too much TV I decide. Younger daughter is beginning to sound like the chief inspector in the police squad room.

"Have you done your homework?" I ask, trying to derail her. "No? Then you'd better get busy. Your last report card looked like the computer got stuck on *D*." It works.

"I got a *B* in 'gets along well with others,'" she defends her record.

"That's great. Colleges are just wild for students who get *B*'s in 'getting along with others.'"

"So what," she says airily. "I'm not going to college, anyway. I'm going to be a mother like you, so I don't have to work."

I wonder. If they know all the facts, will they let me off with justifiable homicide?

"Go do your homework. NOW!"

"You're ducking, mom," older daughter says snidely.

I lunge for her, but she's halfway down the hall, whistling, "If You Tell a Lie, I'll Die."

"Stop that whistling," I yell after her. "Girls who whistle wind up in the House of Good Shepherd." I still kinda believe my mom's story that girls who chew gum or whistle wind up in homes for wayward girls.

I hang on the refrigerator door, trying to figure out what to give the human horde for dinner. I'm afraid to try the hamburger again.

At five o'clock I hear the third questioner stomping the snow off his feet on the front porch. The dogs unwind themselves and stand in straggly line at the door. Two of them jump when it opens. Walter gets banged in the head and howls.

"Hi there, Stanley, Apollo. Sorry about that, Walter. Third time this week isn't it?" He reaches down and scratches heads, and they fall over in a heap at his feet. The girls wait in the living room. They've got the choice spots in front of the fireplace.

He wanders into the kitchen, pulls a Bud from the refrigerator, and leans on the counter watching the carrot peelings swirling down the In-Sink-Erator.

"Think they're getting any better?" he asks.

"Who? The kids or the dogs?" I ask back.

"I know what the kids are doing. I just saw the report cards. I think I'd better have a talk with Miss Sociability tonight."

Stanley wanders into the kitchen and reminds him.

"Who you gonna finish first, Stanley or Apollo?" he asks optimistically.

"Well, there are a lot of things I have to consider," I dodge.

"Like what things?" he prods.

"For one thing, you don't just walk in the ring and say 'Here

I am,'" I say patronizingly. "There are a lot of things. Some judges go for big dogs, some like more elegant ones, some are hung up on a certain color, some are headhunters, some . . ."

"Wait a minute," he interrupts. "What in the hell is a headhunter?"

I pitch the carrots in with the beef roast and wish I'd kept still about headhunters.

"A headhunter is someone who looks only at a dog's head and doesn't care about the rest of the dog." I sound very officious.

He opens another Bud and flips the tab in the trash can. I wish I could send him to do his homework.

"What kind of heads do Stanley and Apollo have?"

I feel another sinking spell coming on.

"Well, Apollo has a very lovely, elegant head." I take a breath and break the news about Stanley. "Stanley has a head like a water bucket."

"Looks like that washes out Stanley," he says.

"No. You just have to learn the ropes," I say.

He goes into the living room, and I can hear him checking the pile.

"Stanley, look at me, fella. By God, you do have a big head." He comes back into the kitchen.

"Then what's good about Stanley?" he inquires.

"He's pretty."

"So is Boo, but nobody ever gave her a blue riboon, except that one time when there weren't any other Bassets."

"That's because I was a novice then. Now I've been to lots of shows, at least ten. I know the ropes now."

I wish I felt as confident as I sounded.

"Go get Miss Sociability and her sister; dinner is ready," I say, rebuffing any further questions for which I have no answers.

Someone in that pile better shape up pretty soon. I'm running out of answers.

19

It was unbelievable that I could have five dogs and not one that was decent enough to show.

Boo was retired. Walter still suffered from Section Eight depression. Aphrodite had stopped growing, not permanently I hoped, but she probably would never be as large as a show bitch should be. Her future would be in motherhood when she was old enough. Then we would have to make another search for a suitable mate. Stanley was still cursed with his overlarge head. Apollo was going through an awkward stage. Between Christmas and the end of February, he'd become a nightmarish collection of parts trying to outgrow each other. He looked eighteen inches tall at the shoulders, more like a Greyhound than a Basset, and his chest had crawled up somewhere even with his chin. All of his ribs stuck out, no matter how much he ate. He looked like the advance man for a famine.

During the lull in Apollo's career while he was pulling himself together, it was necessary to keep him in training, lest we have to begin all over again.

I had a very full program. As soon as the house was presentable after the family's morning exodus, and while the rest of the dogs settled in for "Captain Kangeroo," Apollo and I headed for the basement and daily training sessions. Some days went better than others. On the days he resented being taken away from his programs, we argued a lot.

"The sooner you keep your feet where I put them, the sooner you'll get back upstairs," I'd promise him.

Sometimes it worked, sometimes it didn't. I could have sworn he kept moving them to see how far he could go before I gave up and yelled, "Go ahead. Be a stupid mutt. Make a fool out of yourself at the next show."

I hated it when they played music on one of the programs upstairs while we were gaiting. It seemed to me he was shuffling around in time to the music. Good sense told me dogs do not have a sense of rhythm, but . . .

At least three afternoons a week were spent socializing in shopping malls just to be sure he still loved people. I wondered about the necessity for this, considering the amount of traffic through the house, but I still believed the books with their constant reminders to keep your show dog socially unflappable. Kennel recluses suddenly thrust into the crowded howling dog show world, the books warned, could cause a lot of embarrassment when they tried to run up the walls or cowered between their owners' legs.

Our best socializing, however, was done on Saturday mornings. Apollo was the only dog who attended dancing school on a regular schedule.

The drive from the house to dancing school was punctuated by much complaining from the back seat.

"Mother, he wiped his mouth on my leotards again."

"Then keep your coat closed."

"Then he wipes his mouth on my coat, and I have to wear it to school with dog spit all over it."

"Apollo, turn around and look out the back window," I'd try to conciliate, before open warfare broke out.

Apollo would try to shift and the other would-be-dancer would howl, "Now he's shedding all over me. It sticks to my face and makes me itch."

"Take a Kleenex and wipe it off."

She always acted as if a few dog hairs would leave her face permanently coated with fur.

There would be a quiet interval while they consulted. Out of the corner of my eye, I'd catch a glimpse of two front paws on the back of the seat beside me. They were hoisting seventy pounds of Basset Hound over the seat.

"Don't do that while I'm driving," I'd yell, but it was too late. Propelled from behind Apollo would slither down the seat back. When he was lucky, he landed on the seat. When he missed, he wound up somewhere on the floor with his head on top of my right foot. We caused a lot of excitement among the other drivers when we suddenly shot forward at forty-five miles an hour instead of a sedate thirty-five.

Dancing school was excellent training for Apollo. I hoped the racket of sixteen little girls all tap dancing more or less together to a pianist belting out "Alexander's Rag Time Band" would make him impervious to the din of a dog show. The plan worked. A building could collapse on Apollo, and if he wasn't killed, he'd brush himself off and not quiver.

I think he enjoyed the half-hour of ballet more than the tap dancing. It was quieter, and he seemed to enjoy the sixteen fluttery little girls bobbing and swaying like crippled butterflies. He also preferred Tchaikovsky's "Sugar Plum Fairies" to "Alexander's Rag Time Band." I couldn't find much difference myself between the piano player's renditions.

It didn't seem fair after his faithful attendence to make him miss the recital, but the public school auditorium was strictly off limits to dogs, even those who had attended dancing school.

As winter began loosening its grip, he began shaping up. I could feel little threads of hope inside me as I watched the changes slowly taking place. I measured Apollo, to make sure I wasn't seeing just what I wanted to see, and he really was a very acceptable twelve and one-half inches at the shoulder. His chest had finally settled down and looked like the prow of a proud sailing ship. His ribs had disappeared under a sleek coating of muscle that rippled smoothly when he moved. And when he moved, oh how beautifully he moved.

Front legs that kept reaching out as if there weren't enough ground in the world for him to cover. Hind quarters that drove him forward so easily he seemed to be floating rather than striding. I knew, deep in my heart, I would be blessed only once in my lifetime with one who moved so gracefully, so effortlessly.

Of all the changes, I thanked God, his elegant head had not changed. He looked out at the world from under velvety rows of brow wrinkles. His eyes were the rich brown, almost black, that are so desirable in the Basset Hound breed, and his nostrils were coal black. Most of all, he had about him the quiet dignity that maturity had brought. In him was the noble elegance of the 700 years of breeding behind him.

I dared to hope. Maybe, I told myself, maybe I *had* bred a good one of my own.

Spring came and we hit the dog show road together again.

20

I think Apollo knew. Sometime during the long winter layoff from showing, he had matured from puppy exuberance to grown up poise. We were still a long way from perfect, or for that matter a polished performance, but at least we were now doing things together most of the time.

I finally broke down and let Apollo have the rubber matting (put down at indoor shows to give the dogs firm footing while gaiting) when we gaited, instead of gaiting myself on it. After all, it was there for the dogs.

He reciprocated by improving his turns at the corners. Instead of his previous impersonations of a ship with its mainmast shot away, we were making the turns with only a moderate list on his part. He only whined when I took his chewies away from him before we went into the ring, and the slumping was down to more leaning than slumping. He still had one holdover trick from his puppy days that he'd spring on me every time he thought he'd lulled me into a sense of security. The moment I relaxed, he'd rev up his motor and we'd be off like A. J. Foyt at Daytona. Some of the other exhibitors got the idea we were the pace car for the gaiting. With Apollo you never let down your guard.

We were the first ones into the ring, and we stood quietly waiting for the others to line up behind us. It was being held outdoors, and Apollo sniffed the dew-soaked grass and tried to follow the scent of some long-disappeared bunny under the ring fence. I yanked him back. Disgruntled, he flopped in the wet grass and stretched out as though he were at home in front of the TV. My heart sank as I thought, this is going to be one of *those* days again. I looked at the row of raring-to-go dogs behind me and pulled my semicomatose partner upright. We had a short conversation about the consequences of any nonsense from him today, and he started looking alive.

We moved around the ring smoothly, once, twice, three times. I began to wonder if the judge had forgotten to stop us. After the long winter layoff, my calves were beginning to ache. We stopped finally, and the individual examinations began. I prayed Apollo wouldn't collapse when the judge asked me to let Apollo stand on his own. I whispered one final promise of a mountain of chewies and stood back. Our hours of practice worked. Unless it was that he was frozen by the sight of the judge's tie, with its rows of fierce-looking Doberman Pinschers glaring out at him.

I waited in an agony of fear that Apollo would suddenly slide limply to the ground and lie there looking up at the judge. He was capable of it. When the judge finally moved away from us, I felt spongy inside. Then he gaited us alone and gaited us again. My heart sank.

"Good God," I mumbled under my breath, "is Apollo doing something rotten and I can't see it?" We obeyed the judge's hand as he waved us back to our place in line. We waited.

The rest of the world was blotted out. I felt as though I'd been inside this grassy enclosure forever and would remain here forever. We waited. Numbly, I heard the judge's voice telling us to begin gaiting around the ring again. I knew these were the final moments before he would raise his hand, point to one of the moving dogs, and say the words that all our efforts had been directed toward. I heard the high-pitched yapping of a dog in another ring somewhere. It could have been the whine of a comet coming toward the earth, and it wouldn't have mattered.

When the judge made his choice, I neither saw nor heard. Someone touched me on the shoulder and said, "You can stop now, you've won."

And they laughed at my confusion.

I took Apollo's first blue ribbon and somehow got my senses together enough to mumble a thank you to the judge. Together Apollo and I floated out of the ring.

Fortunately at dog shows no one thinks you're crazy when you kiss a dog.

I couldn't wait with the news. Over the long distance phone I

74

babbled, "We won, we won, we won. Me and Apollo, we won . . . Of course I'll drive carefully."

Apollo and I found a shady spot on the grass and shared lunch. Together we munched on the half-steamed hot dogs and soggy buns, but today they tasted like ambrosia. We toasted our win in lukewarm orange drink. It could have been Dom Perignon. Blue ribbons are very magic things.

I drove home very carefully. I was driving the very best dog in the world.

Three more weekends passed in quick succession. Apollo won two times out of three, and I generously excused the one poor soul who hadn't been able to tell he was the best dog in the world.

We had three blue ribbons, a silver bowl, a silver butter dish, and a twelve-inch naked angel on a walnut base. I began counting up those all important points he needed to become a champion. We needed fifteen. We had seven.

I could already see that championship certificate hanging on my wall at home. I would take the certificate into Mr. Herlihy; he did the best framing in town, and I wouldn't care how much he charged. All my dreams were possible now.

Then I learned. Never trust man's best friend.

21

I had us booked solid for four more weekends. Then out of the blue, the hunger strike started.

Not once in their entire lives had one of them missed a meal. They were ready to eat anytime, anyplace, anything that wouldn't eat them first. Then Apollo quit eating.

The first day when he passed, I didn't worry too much. He's probably got a cache of chewies he's living off secretly, I told myself. I kept an eye on him all day hoping he'd lead me to them.

The second day when he passed again, I started getting worked up.

"What's the matter with you? Think you're too good to eat with the horde now that you've got a few ribbons?" I asked snottily, hoping to shake him up. He gave me a disgusted look and clumped out of the kitchen. Everybody else was eating like flood victims with their first Care package. I was puzzled.

"Walter, get your head out of the dish a sec," I ordered, pushing his head to one side and grabbing his pan. I sniffed the few crumbs in the bottom and then cross-checked with Apollo's pan. The smells were identical, except Walter was having a recurrence of his halitosis.

"You're going to have to have your teeth cleaned again, Walter," I said, absentmindedly giving him Apollo's full pan. Walter downed the full pan like Moses had just ordered up more manna from Heaven. Gloomily I picked up the scoured-clean pans from the rest of them and wandered into the living room where Apollo was stretched out.

"Today's Tuesday," I said. "You've got four more days before Sunday's show to get your head straightened out about this eating thing."

I tossed him a test chewy, and he rolled it under the couch. We were in trouble. Two days into a hunger strike and his ribs were beginning to show again. By Sunday he'd look like a Relief for Bangladesh poster.

I swung into action. I switched dog foods. Maybe he was bored with the same old menu every day. I mixed up a special bowl of Crunchies, the dog food even the finickiest eater will adore. He took one sniff and gagged.

The rest of them finished up the bag of Crunchies the next day and moaned for more.

I whipped through all the books and magazines for special diets. I never dreamed there were so many diets for canines. Someone had thought of everything that could possibly interfere with the proper nourishment of our four-footed friends. There were diets for prenatal mothers, postnatal mothers, lactating mothers, poorly performing stud dogs, overanxious stud dogs, dogs with poor coats, dogs with spotty coat problems (it promised to grow hair in the deficient areas only), constipated dogs, and those at the other end of the spectrum with what is delicately referred to as the loose-stool syndrome. (This diet promised the finest stools you'll ever pick up in your dog runs. It sounded a little heavy on the bone meal and cautioned not to be concerned if the stools seemed to be a strange bleached white color.)

One caught my fancy. It promised rather grandly that feeding your apricot Poodle daily rations of carrots would deepen his apricot color smashingly. Gee, I thought, same deal as the red beets and the flamingos at the zoo.

I finally found what I was looking for. It was something labeled, "Specially Good for That Specially Good Pal." Apollo and I weren't even on speaking terms, but I buried my animosity for a last-ditch try. It took an extra trip to the grocers and put a dent in my household money, but I'd make it up on something else. Maybe I'd try using only a half cup of detergent per washer load.

Apollo is probably the world's only dog who turned up his nose at ground beef heart sauteed with fresh scallions, barely boiled wild rice, and pearl barley with a smidgin of baby carrots grated over the top.

The place still smelled enticing at five-thirty, when the human horde gathered for dinner.

"Boy, something sure smells good," father said, gloating in anticipation.

"We gonna have company tonight?" younger daughter asked.

"You think it only smells good in here when we have company?" I barked at her, trying to back her off before she started rooting in the trash to see what she was missing. I knew I should have thrown that wild rice box out in the big trash can.

"How come it smells so good and we're having old hamburgers again?" Older daughter was suspicious. Her normal state. I felt sorry for whoever decided to marry her.

"Did you have company for lunch?" father asked, munching on his hamburger.

"What is this? Twenty Questions? Why don't all of you just eat and keep quiet? You're getting on my nerves," I said peevishly.

On day three of the hunger strike, I tried force feeding his highness. I'd never tried force feeding before. First, because around our place it was about as necessary as sprinkling the grass in January. Second, it always seemed indecent to force food on an unwilling animal.

But desperate conditions called for desperate measures. The finicky eaters' section in Canine Cookery said, "Make little ballies by rolling wet dog food into walnut-sized hunks, and then slide smoothly down the throat." I made piles of the walnut-sized ballies and called Apollo into the kitchen. Stanley, who had been watching the preparations, was slavering in anticipation when I chased him out of the kitchen. I took Stanley's approval as a good sign for what was coming. Hopefully I held the plate of ballies under Apollo's nose for one last chance to eat on his own, muttered an appeal to the Mother of Perpetual Help, and waited. They both turned me down.

The book didn't explain how you forced food down a dog who insisted on lying either on his side or flat on his back with all four feet stuck stiffly up in the air. Their test-kitchen dogs must have been in the same state as the lions before they threw the Christians to them. Apollo would have helped the Christians escape.

I yanked him partway to his feet to take the S curve out of his esophagus, pried open his mouth, and popped in one of my ballies.

His performance was the greatest thing since James Cagney

gave up death scenes in gangster films. He stiffened, his eyes bulged, he staggered drunkenly around the kitchen. I thought one time I saw him clutch his throat, but that was hardly possible. He gagged, he made choking sounds, he rattled and reeled around the floor a couple more times before he finished up in a heap alongside the back door. He lay there looking up at me accusingly. I waited for him to murmur hoarsely, "Tell mom I'm sorry for all the trouble I caused her." He closed his eyes, and I nearly collapsed on top of his prone body.

Now you've done it, I berated myself. You've killed your own dog. That's all he meant to you, just something you could use to feed your ego with on Sunday mornings. You don't really love dogs. Oh please, God, I promised, let him live and I'll never do it again.

From under the wrinkles, I thought I caught a glimpse of a brown eye looking at me. I looked closer. He *was* looking at me.

"Alright Cagney, on your feet," I screeched at him. "You're going to the vet."

Once the vet saw it wasn't Walter, his greeting was warm.

"Hi there, fella," he said as he shoved the thermometer in Apollo's rear aperture.

"Do you ever lose one of those?" I questioned curiously.

"Every once in a while," he answered blithely.

"What happens when you lose one?"

"I just add it on the bill," he said, enjoying one of his trade jokes.

"Well, wouldja keep an eye on that one, please?" I asked. "I've already got enough trouble with him."

After he removed the thermometer, he listened as I explained the problem.

"He's stopped eating."

"For how long?"

"Since Tuesday."

He picked up what was left of the fat on Apollo's rump.

"He could go for a month on what he's got stored here," he said.

"That's loose skin, not fat," I argued.

"He'll eat when he's hungry," was the unsatisfactory answer.

"Listen, he's a show dog," I explained. "Couldn't I have some appetite pepper-uppers until he gets started again?" I knew it was like asking for the keys to his new sports car sitting out back. He was dead set against medicating unless it was necessary.

"He looks fine to me. Temperature's normal, soft tissue looks healthy, eyes are clear."

"How long do you think he'll stay that way if he doesn't eat?"

"I've never seen a dog starve to death with food around. He'll eat when he's hungry."

"No pills?"

"No pills."

I dragged stringy past the curious stares of the others waiting their turn. From behind me I could hear the vet still talking.

"Next time you bring Walter in, tell him to leave his friends outside."

I clenched my teeth. Very funny.

After dinner I slumped on the couch. A rough guess was that Apollo had lost five pounds today, or at least he looked five pounds lighter.

"Everything all set for Sunday?" my husband inquired cheerfully.

"We're not going anywhere Sunday. Look at that string-bean," I said, pointing a toe at Apollo, busy shoving his pile of chewies under a chair.

Apollo was satisfied that the chewies were safely stowed away and took a few turns around the room to show off his new slim trim figure.

"He does look a little scroungy," he agreed.

"He's going on the back burner until he comes to his senses."

"How about Stanley?"

"Stanley?"

"You said Stanley was your second choice until Aphrodite gets herself together," he reminded me.

"Stand up, Stanley," I commanded the hulk at the bottom of the pile. "Oh God!" I whimpered. "Stanley, turn your head sideways." Stanley continued to stare at me full face, his tail wagging furiously. He was thrilled at being the main attraction.

"Look at his head," I whimpered again.

"When he hangs it, it doesn't look too bad," he tried to console me. Stanley looked like he was two feet wide between his ears.

Stanley hobbled over—one of his feet was asleep—and lay his sticky muzzle in my lap. I rubbed his head absently.

80

"Maybe if I put a sack over his head . . ." I mused.

"You'll need a leaves-and-grass bag to fit him," he joked.

Stanley was getting stoned on all this attention. He slumped to the carpet like a beached whale.

He never got his chance. Stanley's career was nipped in the bud when we unexpectedly became the pariahs of Sherwood Meadows subdivision.

22

The final melt of an unexpected spring snowfall was gurgling in the gutters the day one of the local constabulary appeared on our front porch.

Except for an occasional drive through the subdivision's streets to check out a complaint that some teenager was racing his car, or that the trash collectors were leaving more trash in the streets than they carried away, the Boltonville police force seldom visited Sherwood Meadows.

The patrol car parked smack in front of 722 Tilbury Walk, and the uniformed figure on my front porch caused an immediate stir among the neat row of middle-management split levels. The occupants of four houses on either side of ours were suddenly attacked by a need to sweep their walks. The last of the winter's soggy leaves were flying before their brooms as I opened the front door.

"Good morning. I'm Officer Delman Watson," he introduced himself.

"I know who you are, Del. I just saw you night before last at the PTA meeting," I reminded him.

Office Delman Watson made it clear being PTA buddies didn't count when he was on official business.

"Are you the party permanently residing at 722 Tilbury Walk?"

I nodded my head agreeably. He knew I lived here. His kids played with mine.

He made a couple of official-looking check marks in his book. It was beginning to dawn on me why he was here. The sweepers were edging closer, so I invited him inside the house. In seconds I realized my mistake when five hounds surrounded us while

Officer Watson began reading Boltonville's Ordinance S-126-J, Livestock Regulations, Section C. "No more than three adult dogs and any number of puppies up to three months of age are permitted per household."

"You understand that Sherwood Meadows subdivision is within the town limits of Boltonville?" he asked.

Of course I know that. We paid enough taxes every January 1st to Boltonville to know where we lived.

"Of course I know we live in Boltonville, Del," I said.

Then the ax fell.

"We have received a complaint that you have more dogs than the legal limit. I'm here to investigate the complaint," he said.

Well, I thought to myself, he isn't going to have much investigating to do with five hounds fawning at his feet. I admitted that, yes, we did have five dogs.

"Are any of them under three months of age?" he inquired.

I detected a tiny note of hope in his question and wished I could help, but there is no way to palm off a sixty- to seventy-pound Basset Hound as a three-month-old puppy. Even Aphrodite, who disappointingly hadn't grown an inch since she was six months old, was still a little too much to pass off as a puppy.

"No," I admitted ruefully. "They're all over three months."

He seemed disappointed.

Five entranced hounds and one disturbed human listened attentively as he delivered Boltonville's ultimatum: Either cut back to the legal limit or find another place to live. As he was delivering the ultimatum, three of the fool hounds were trying to lick the shine off his shoes. I wanted to kick them.

"How come nobody ever complains about the cats?" I inquired. "With all the yowling that goes on at night around here, it sounds like there must be ten cats per family, but nobody hollers about that I guess."

"If we receive a complaint, we'll investigate," he said.

"Oh, sure."

After a few moments of stiff silence, I led him to the door, with the fools following him and falling all over themselves being friendly. After he left, I berated them. "You're the only dummies in the world who would fall in love with your executioner."

As he made his way back to the patrol car, the sweepers were reversing their direction and sweeping the leaves back to where they'd started before the excitement began. Among them was the Judas who had betrayed us.

Lying in bed that night, I heard the wind whipping around the corner of the house. I smiled in small revenge. By morning the sweepers' leaves would be scattered all over their spic and span sidewalks again.

23

On June first we departed convenient suburbia for farther out, inconvenient suburbia, where neighbors took a more sanguine view of livestock.

The move took us to three acres with nice trees and an aging, nondescript farmhouse, built with typical midwestern lack of imagination. The rooms were old-fashioned and large and featured costly heat loss in the form of twelve-foot ceilings. There were only two real disaster areas. The entry hall was wallpapered in flocks of black ducks winging their way into a fiery orange sunset. I decided it would have to go. The kitchen was a heartbreaker. It was fourteen by twenty feet of solid fingermarked aqua paint. Nothing had been spared. The cabinets had a molasses-thick coating of it, the ceiling, the baseboards, even the light fixture, had its share of aqua paint. Only the floor had escaped the madman's brush. It was a greasy gray with a bloody-red spatter pattern that shrieked of murders most foul. It, too, would have to go.

I fervently hoped that everybody on Tilbury Walk got sod worms in their lawns this summer.

The hounds accepted their new quarters as soon as they located the fieldstone fireplace, which was large enough to roast a small ox. In the middle of an early summer heat wave, they needed the reassurance of a steady heat supply for when winter's ice gnomes came marching across the Midwest again.

We consoled ourselves with promises that the place had possibilities, whenever the finances became available. I visualized the three acres with a snappy kennel building and chain link runs and a *non-aqua* kitchen. But until better times we'd continue to live in cozy togetherness.

The sudden shift from convenient suburbia caused some

minor hassles among the humans. The family provider couldn't get his driving schedule arranged and either got to his office two hours before anyone else or missed the first three clients of the day.

The kids missed everything, even the kids they hadn't liked in Boltonville. They spent a lot of time trying to kill each other out of sheer boredom. Twenty miles from the city limits isn't exactly rural America, but the family was acting as if we'd returned to the Stone Age.

In the melee of moving, I didn't dare mention dog shows. Apollo was eating again like he thought the world's supply of food would disappear at midnight. I restrained myself from breaking his neck. When things settled down again, I consoled myself, we'd get started showing.

The new place had another difference from the well-ordered routine of Sherwood Meadows. After word got around that new people were living in the old farmhouse, we had a steady stream of little people moving through the place. All day long, Sundays included, these small gypsies caravanned in the front door, marched into the kitchen, and announced, "I need a drink of water," or "I gotta go potty," and then, mission accomplished, flitted out the back door. Elbow deep in peach butter (the place had six peach trees) for next winter's breakfast toast, or sewing up nylon net tutus for next month's dance recital, I mostly ignored the comings and goings, except for an occasional interruption when a Too-Short-for-the-Door-Knob would insist, "You'd better hurry up, or I'll wet my pants." They had the notion I cared if they wet their pants. Occasionally, I trapped one for questioning when it got its underwear caught in its pants' zipper.

"Why does everybody stop here to go to the bathroom? Don't you kids have homes?" I'd ask, as I was trying to separate the zipper from size-two Doctor Dentons.

"Yeth, but it'th too far," was the excuse.

"If it's that far, then how did you get here in the first place? Fly?"

The idea of flying always seemed to bring on an attack of self-conscious giggles.

"Then you take the same plane you came in on the next time you have to go," I'd warn. "I'm too busy to stop and bother with you."

They giggled some more and banged out the door.

Some of them were also food critics. One little myopic soul finished his pottying and then sashayed over to the sink where I was still smushing around with the peach butter. I tried ignoring him while he chinned himself on the sink.

"What's that stuff?" he wanted to know.

"It's peach butter," I said, offering him a taste.

"YIK! I wouldn't eat that stuff," he spluttered.

"Don't worry," I said, "You're not on my guest list for breakfast."

I felt better now that I had squelched at least one of the food critics.

The mystery of where they came from was finally solved when I discovered we were exactly at the halfway point between the playground and the new housing development hidden behind the hill that sloped up from our property in back of the house. I also solved the mystery of the erratic toilet habits the hounds had developed. They were taking advantage of the steady door openings to zip in and out. It avoided having to endure the outdoors, which they still hated, until I was satisfied with their performance. Also, they were making it very plain that they missed the air-conditioned comfort of their former home by shedding ceaselessly.

Between shedding and whining, they bellied themselves across the floor searching for cool spots on the tiles. The only ones who seemed halfway comfortable were the ones who had picked up raging cases of grass eczema and had huge bald spots. Apollo was a total wreck again. From skinny and furry he'd turned fat and nearly bald. He had the worst case of summer grass eczema the vet had ever seen. I wondered what other catastrophe could stymie my efforts to raise my own champion.

24

By the end of summer, we were up to four rolls of "squeezably soft" per week in the downstairs bathroom. My kennel-building fund was going to the grocer for toilet tissue. I dreaded seeing the water bill for the drinking and flushing that seemed to peak in the soggy heat of August. I hoped the Boltonville trees had been invaded by swarms of eastern tent caterpillers.

The beginning of school saw no letup in the heat, but it did cut down on the midday trafficking through the house. The hounds, without their door-openers, were back on their crummy schedule of waiting until I was on the phone or in the shower before deciding their kidneys were on red alert. Between the alerts they mostly crawled around the floor slobbering and scratching their bald spots.

The quiet ended and business picked up again when the school bus disgorged its load right smack in front of our house. I was reasonably sure the school had water fountains and bathrooms, but we still held our position as the caravan oasis between school and home behind the hill.

With the onset of the boots and the snowsuit season, I launched a determined effort against kids and hounds. I took on the kids first. Except for absolute emergencies, they were told firmly, "Go home and use your own bathroom. I don't have time to wrestle you out of your Captain Marvel space snowsuits."

Some took the hint and gave up. For the few incorrigibles, as a final resort, I hung a sign on the front door:

BATHROOM CLOSED UNTIL SPRING

A few still hung around on the front porch hoping I'd relent or threatening to wet their pants, but after it turned really cold,

89

even the most inveterate pants-wetters began passing the house.

My hopes had begun rising again. The bald spots were filled in, Apollo's ribs had receded beneath a comforting coating of fat, and I was panting to get back out again.

If we put on a really determined drive, we could have a champion under the Christmas tree.

The entry forms were coming in and going back out again until the check book began looking like we were singlehandedly supporting all the kennel club treasuries within a 200-mile radius. A mileage limitation was imposed to avoid costly overnight stays at motels. I envied all those plush vans and their smug owners who were sleeping like angels while I was ploughing my way down the highways as the birds rubbed the sleep from their eyes.

If I envied the van owners, I was developing a desire to apply thumb screws or iron maidens to those helpful souls who drew the maps that were *supposed* to lead you right into the Bootstrap County fairgrounds.

The night before, I'd sit and study those homemade messes of squiggly lines that looked more like dessicated spiders than maps. While Apollo recovered from the shock of another immersion in his hated tin tub, I'd try to figure out how to get us there in the morning without winding up in New Orleans or Winnemukee, Wisconsin. I was pretty certain the folks who had drawn the maps were locals who never left their homes in Bootstrap County and knew the territory intimately.

They had another dandy trick. The homemade maps would tell you, "Ramp off at Exit 84, County Road 141. Come 20 miles to show site." Besides the embarrassment, it is also dangerous to sit at the top of Ramp 84 with five fully-loaded, impatient tractor-trailers waiting behind you while you're deciding which direction they meant on County Road 141. Please, God, I'd pray, let just one car with dogs pass so I can follow it.

Apollo and I were arriving at the shows by the skin of our teeth. We were following those squiggly lines from one country town to another or spending too much time sitting at the top of ramps. We missed one show entirely because I followed a car full of dogs and wound up at the Macoupin County Animal Shelter. Thank You, God, for nothing, I muttered, as I rolled 150 weary miles back home and then tried to explain how I'd managed to wind up at an animal shelter instead of a dog show.

In spite of the obstacles of bad maps and obscure locations, we did manage to pick up more points. Then, just two points short of our goal, the roof fell in again. Unbelievably, Apollo was turning into a shambles before my eyes. I owned the only dog on the North American continent who was shedding like crazy in mid-November. And he was getting millions of little red spots all over his body. I could have sworn he was doing it to avoid taking another bath.

We hustled back to the vet's, but at least this time I had a legitimate disease.

"Wouldja look at this miserable dog?" I wailed.

"Looks awful, doesn't he," he agreed for once.

He scraped and Apollo howled; he squinted into his microscope, and Apollo shed fur all over his examining table.

"Stop shedding," I said. "You'll get pneumonia when we go outside." He clawed another half-bucket of fur off his flanks.

"He's got dermatitis, but it's not catching," he said through the clouds of dog hair floating around the examining room.

"How long does it last?" I asked.

"Depends on how well it responds," he hedged.

"Well, can't you check your books or something? I'd like to know," I said irritably.

He ignored my pushing and kept on counting pills, filling a bottle with some clear liquid that was mainly to keep me happy, and filling another bottle with some creamy-looking shampoo. He'd learned early in his practice that humans were only satisfied when they had something to smear on skin complaints. It wasn't going to last on Apollo's hide for three minutes when the rest of the dogs got their first taste of him.

"Will that stuff give them diarrhea?" I wanted to know.

"Only if he takes it straight from the bottle."

"The rest of them are going to lick it off him," I warned.

Without a word he reached into the cabinet and added a couple of drops of something else to the rubbing compound.

"Wanna bet they don't touch him now?" he said complacently.

He plunged enough of some milky white liquid into Apollo's rump to cure an advanced case of jungle rot and headed us toward the door. At every step more clouds of his fast-disappearing coat swirled around us.

"Will he be okay in about two weeks?" I asked hopefully.

"No."

"Three weeks?"

"He'll be better."

"Look, you're going to have to do better than this," I said grimly.

"Don't worry. In three or four weeks, his coat will start coming in again. Couple of weeks after that, he'll be good as new."

"Couple of weeks! My God, that's Christmas."

"Sure will be," he said affably and deftly shoved Apollo out the door to scratch on the sidewalk.

"Alright, dummy, get in the car," I said while I boosted his bare rump into the car.

He settled back on the seat alongside me and listened as I continued crabbing at him and a world that seemed determined to frustrate my plans.

The first few snowflakes began hitting the windshield. He leaned his muzzle up against the window trying to lick the flakes off the glass, and I could almost swear he was smiling.

No more getting prodded out of his sleep for long drives to shows until springtime.

I flipped on the wipers and drove home morosely.

No Christmas champion under the tree.

25

It began snowing on the fifteenth of November, and it acted as if it intended to snow straight through till the fifteenth of April. Every day it snowed a little or a lot. Mostly a lot.

At first I enjoyed the sort of rustic charm of the snow sifting down, quietly covering the dead grass and coating the leafless trees. The rustic charm began wearing thin when it began to look like the snow god had gone berserk. My mood turned from quiet wonder to ugly when every day I faced the job of staggering outside, grabbing a shovel, and digging a path from the front door to the road. The road seemed to move farther away from the house every time I shoveled. My disposition wasn't improved whenever I glanced up from the shoveling and beheld five pairs of eyes lined up at the windows, fascinated at the sight of me floundering around in hip-deep drifts. They thoroughly enjoyed the daily entertainment.

They were leading a life of complete serenity. Plenty of good food, a regular supply of chewies, new programs on TV, and plenty of logs on the fire. The only flaw in their existence was the mandatory three trips daily to the outside for relieving the accumulation of good food and chewies. As the snow deepened and the winds grew colder, the daily sessions began taking on the looks of the running of the bulls at Pamplona.

It would start with me hustling them out of their corners, off the furniture, and out from under the beds where some of the brighter ones would take refuge when they saw me coming. Once I'd managed to round them up and had the troops poised, with the dumber ones in the front row, I'd try whipping up their courage with clever remarks.

"Wait until you see all the bunnies outside," I'd challenge their sporting instincts. For those who weren't interested in

93

bunnies, I'd do my imitation of a pussy cat. That always drove Walter wild, but not wild enough to go outside voluntarily. My efforts usually merited a response of everybody eyeing me glumly. They had heard all of this before and knew there were no bunnies or anything else in its right mind outside in this weather. But like it or not, I was running the show, and they *were* going outside.

Once the door was opened and the first blast of freezing air hit them, the passive resistance turned to outright panic and rebellion. Even the dummies in the front row who had been leaning toward the door knew it was very bad out there. They began shoving toward the rear and colliding with those in the back row who were being urged forward by my foot pushing against their rumps. Before you could say "Jack Robinson," it would turn into a weaving, plunging mass of dogs trying to move in opposite directions and me trying to shove the whole milling mass outside and slam the door shut.

Frequently, petty bickering broke out. Somebody had his big foot on somebody else's ear, or one of the males, seeing his chance in the general uproar, would try to interject some sex into the goings-on. He'd get nipped for his cravenness and then set up an offended howling until he saw another chance. The battle surged back and forth until someone in the front line would finally break, and everybody tumbled out onto the porch.

Before they could retreat, I'd slam the door. Once in a while, a slow mover wouldn't quite clear the door before it closed and would get rapped smartly by it for lagging, which brought on more anguished howling from the victim. From the safety of the inside, I'd warn unsympathetically, "Whether you're in the door or out, it closes in five seconds."

The brighter ones recognized when all hope was gone and slithered down the steps, took care of things, and were poised on the porch for the reopening. The really recalcitrant ones would hang around forlornly on the porch, hoping I wouldn't notice. They'd lounge against the door, trying to soak up any heat that escaped through the cracks, and gaze dejectedly at the belly-deep snow covering the yard until I kicked the door a few times at about the spot where I thought their heads would be.

"Either get down there and do it, or you'll stay out there until you freeze to death," I'd yell through the door.

Disgustedly, they'd slide down the steps, plunge into the

snow, and hustle around trying to act businesslike enough to satisfy me. It was hard to tell if they were serious or just killing time until I relented and opened the door again. In the deep snow, their plumbing was out of sight.

When they trooped back inside shivering and shaking wet snow all over the kitchen floor, they were snotty about my offers of friendship. They accepted their chewy rewards for good conduct grudgingly and stalked out of the kitchen, all injured dignity. Until the next roundup.

By mid-January we were all exhausted with rustic charm. The snow kept falling and the wind kept howling as we sank deeper and deeper into winter apathy. Apollo was a constant source of irritation. His coat looked smashing. The deeper the snow got the better he looked. I felt like painting "I need two points" on his sides and running him down the road. I resigned myself to having an Easter champion.

It was near the end of January when they finally got their revenge on me for the daily forced dances with the snow fairies.

I should have suspected something was up when, instead of the usual sounds of whining and thumping against the back-door, everything was deadly quiet. I laid out the chewies on the counter, turned up the burner under the pot of vegetable soup on the stove—a sort of homey touch for the homecoming of my brave family who had mushed off to their daily chores at office and school—and opened the door expecting the usual onslaught of wet dogs. Instead, the porch was empty, not a dog in sight. I looked out over their usual haunts and caught a glimpse of the backside of the last one disappearing over the snow fence. Dear God! They'd used the piled-up snow as a ramp and had escaped into the field behind the fence.

"You miserable wretches," I screamed at the empty yard.

I began grabbing up the various parts of my shoveling outfit. The hooded parka was a size-forty relic that my husband had abandoned after his one and only hunting trip years before. He'd chickened out when the duck he'd shot cast an accusing glance at him before it expired. Besides being five sizes too large, the parka had torn pockets that let in cold air and a rusty zipper with so many teeth missing that it burst open at the slightest exertion on my part. The hood was useless. Its fake fur lining had supplied food for a horde of moths that loved its taste. To keep my head from turning into a giant ice ball, I wrapped it in two itchy woolen scarves that sent waves of moth ball scent past my nose and nearly asphyxiated me. Half-crazy with fear, I yanked on husband's size-eleven rubber waders and flung myself out the door in pursuit of the escapees.

I tore up the same ramp of packed snow they'd escaped on and fell flat on my face in the soft snow on the other side. I was sure I was a goner as I sank in the fluffy stuff and the world was blotted out. Weighted down by my ragbag suit of armor, I was in the same disastrous position as an unhorsed knight. I struggled and managed finally to push myself upright. For a weird moment I remembered how as children we used to make snow angels by flopping down in the snow and waving our arms back and forth. I forgot about snow angels when I looked out across the field and saw nothing but unblemished snow.

There wasn't a dog or a dog track to be seen. My God, I thought, how far could they get in this stuff. Then a worse possibility hit me. They hadn't gone anywhere. They were buried somewhere beneath this avalanche of white stuff. They had hit the other side like I had and sunk out of sight. I couldn't

even see the marks where they had vanished.

I swept back and forth in snowy circles, calling, watching for movements, poking my arm down into the piled-up drifts. There should be some trace, at least a disturbed spot, where they'd fallen in. Three hundred pounds of dog couldn't disappear without disturbing something. I strained, but I couldn't see a rotten thing except where I'd been mucking around and where I'd fallen and made a snow angel. My hands were freezing up to the elbows, the zipper had popped open when I'd done my swan dive into the snow, and the cold air was driving in and turning me into an icicle. The waders were so full of snow I could barely move my feet. I was engulfed in total despair.

"AW, COME ON, GOD," I bellowed into the frozen air. "Help me find them."

God must have been aboard a cruise ship in the Bahamas. The only answer I got was more cold wind and a runny nose.

I plunged back and forth, poking, trying to feel something beneath the damned snow. I rubbed the snowy sleeve of the parka across my runny nose and got a face full of snow.

"Okay, God. You made them. They're Your creatures. You made them. If You don't care, neither do I," I said despondently and headed back over the fence and down the ramp. The tears were streaming down my half-frozen face. I had lost one of the waders and hobbled across the yard like a flamingo with a broken leg. I shoved the door open and threw myself on the kitchen floor and blubbered.

All my beautiful babies and their beautiful mother were buried somewhere out there in a snowy tomb. And God didn't even care.

I barely heard the first thump, then another, then one a little louder, and finally a raucous medley of familiar whining and howling.

"Oh God!" I mumbled to myself. "They've turned into haunts already." We'd never be able to stay in this house.

I listened. Haunts might thump and howl, but haunts didn't bark and scratch on doors.

I shot through the hall to the front door and flung it open. All five plunged in, spraying snow and mud halfway up the flying ducks wallpaper. They made a beeline for the fireplace and practically threw themselves on top of the burning logs. I followed, counting to make sure they were all there, and the relief began welling up inside me.

The relief subsided and was followed by a growing curiosity. Exactly where had they gone, I wondered. They couldn't have fallen into the snow as I had. There were no holes in the snow. I refused to accept the idea they could have walked over the snow. Even Jesus had only been able to manage that trick on water. Mud? They were muddy. A light began flashing in my head. It was becoming clearer now.

They had gone up the ramp, saw what was on the other side, couldn't back down because the others were behind, and had simply slipped off to the side and followed the creek bed alongside the fence, where the snow was slushy, to the driveway in front. If I hadn't banged around, I would have seen what had happened. Curiosity turned into a blind rage at the sprawled figures in front of the fireplace. While I'd been out there in a state of hysteria, wallowing around half-frozen and flirting with frostbite, they were all waiting high and dry on the front porch.

I directed an icy stare—or what passed for an icy stare, since my face still felt like I'd gotten too close to a witch burning— and began shouting at the top of my voice.

"This is absolutely your last chance. You're the worst bunch of wretches I've ever had the misfortune to live with. You disgrace me at the vet's, you get kicked out of Obedience School, you get all kinds of rotten diseases, you even managed to screw up my dinner party when you weren't due for another three days. Enough is enough. From now on, I RUN THE SHOW. And may all of you freeze to death if you ever run away from home again."

My chest felt tight, my throat was beginning to burn. On top of everything else, I was coming down with a cold.

"Don't ask me for another chewy for the rest of the night, and start cleaning the mud off of your feet," I croaked at them.

When the family came home, I was stretched out on the couch swigging cough syrup and spraying Neo-Synephrine up my nose.

"God, what a day," he groused. "Couldn't get out of the building for lunch; we had to eat in the cafeteria. And the traffic was terrible. Took almost an hour more than usual to make it out here. Weatherman says more snow tonight."

98

"Thanks for the good news. I was afraid we might run out of snow," I said.

I pushed myself into a sitting position and went into a fit of coughing. My eyeballs felt like they had popped out and were rolling across the floor.

"You oughtta stay out of that snow," he said sympathetically.

"Tell them about it," I said, pointing at the five fat rumps pushed up to the fire.

I coughed and my nose dripped until the last of the snow melted away.

26

I f you'll put the paper down for a minute, there's something I want to talk about," I said to the face hidden from view across the breakfast table.

"I can hear you through the paper," he said.

"I want to see your face," I insisted.

The paper was lowered to half-mast.

"You know," I started, "it's a pain in the neck every time the dogs go outside and I have to hang around and watch them. Wouldn't it be nicer if we just put up a little bit of fence?"

"What's a little bit of fence?" he asked skeptically.

"Well, sort of from where the snow fence was all winter, at the creek, to the end of the house and then zigzag over to the driveway."

He calculated the space I'd described and frowned.

"That's about a quarter of an acre, not counting the zigzags."

"That little bitty space is a quarter of an acre?" I asked incredulously. I've never been able to estimate so much as the size of a room.

"It's not that bad, really," he said, relenting a little.

I jumped at the opening.

"Then could we zag around that big tree, and they could lie under it in the shade?"

"Like they lay around the puppy pen?" he smiled over the top of the paper, knowingly.

"That was because they didn't know about grass then," I defended their dislike of the puppy pen.

"Alright, I'll check around today and see how much they want." He disappeared behind the paper again.

"Please put the paper down. I've got something else."

Just his eyes appeared over the edge of the paper.

"As soon as we get the Easter Bunny out of the way and your parents' anniversary bash and the spring play at school and the weekend you want to clean the leaves out of the gutters, I'd like to start going to the dog shows again." I hadn't realized until that moment what a formidable list had to be gotten out of the way before Apollo and I could resume his interrupted show career.

"Okay by me," he agreed.

As soon as the kitchen was cleared, I checked the calendar. Easter was the second weekend in March. God, I wished they would outgrow those chocolate bunnies. They cost a fortune. The weekend after that, if it didn't rain, he could do his high wire act for cleaning the gutters while I steadied the ladder and ducked the rain of soggy leaves and leftover birds' nests that he pitched down without looking to see if I was underneath. This coming weekend I'd get mom and pop's anniversary bash out of the way. It was a little ahead of schedule, but they wouldn't mind, I hoped.

I sat in the middle of the living room floor digging through the latest issue of the AKC *Gazette,* checking the lists of shows. I hoped there would be one within my driving range for the first weekend in April. I found one, and anticipation welled inside of me, the glow almost filled the room. I couldn't wait to get started again.

The melting snow made plopping sounds as it slid off the roof and hit the ground outside the windows. It was a promise that spring was nearly here. And that the rotten gutters were stopped up again. Please, God, I prayed, hold the rain until we get the gutters cleaned.

In two weeks the fence builders arrived, and I could hardly wait until they finished. Which was a big mistake. I'd had dreams of an immediate rest from the chore of waiting three times a day while the dogs snuffled each piece of grass searching for a virgin piece of ground unsullied by others relieving themselves, but the dreams faded under the lackadaisical performance of the fence builders. They worked as if they intended to spend the entire spring and summer in my backyard. The fence moved forward by inches instead of feet. Every time I looked out, they were either eating lunch, swigging beer, or disappearing over the hill to get rid of the beer they had swigged. I tried shaming them by standing on the porch and staring at them belligerently. The minute I went back inside, they resumed their beer swigging and hill tripping. They could have built a wall around the property from beer cans. I'd about given up on the whole project when they finally set the last pole in place, packed up their gear, and zipped out of the driveway, still swigging as they zoomed onto the road. Miraculously, the fence was on a straight line, even though its builders were not.

For all of my efforts, the hounds weren't any fonder of their new outside quarters than they had been of the puppy pen. But at least now I could let them outside without having to stand and make sure no one decided to run away from home again.

Easter was over, the gutters were cleaned, the school play was scheduled for the last weekend in March. Everything was ready for Apollo and me to go after those last two championship points.

27

In anticipation of returning to the dog show world, I had fulfilled all my tasks admirably. The house had been cleaned of the winter's accumulation of dirt, my interest in cooking had revived, hamburgers were appearing less frequently on the dinner table, and I had stayed up until one o'clock two nights in a row sewing the court costume for Lady Guinevere. Younger daughter had been chosen to play the part in the school play because she had blonde hair.

"For Pete's sake. Are you the only blonde kid in that school?" I'd asked her, as I sewed yards and yards of cheap sateen that should look like satin if you weren't in the first row of seats.

"No, but I can talk the loudest," was her explanation for her rise to stardom. That I could believe. She had a bullhorn for lungs. I never would have made it if older daughter hadn't been chosen to be an old peasant woman. We had plenty of rags around the place to outfit her authentically.

The play came off smoothly. Nobody missed a word that Lady Guinevere said, and the old peasant woman was suitably ragged. I breathed a sigh of relief and went home safe in my belief that now it was my turn.

God rewards the just. He also tries men's souls. I knew He was still mad at me for being sassy during the great escape. Aphrodite came "in season."

There is nothing in this world, or any other, that can compare to the energy and volume of sound put out by three male dogs in their prime and in the throes of unrequited love. For the twenty-one days of a bitch's heat season, they become perpetual motion machines.

Aphrodite did not inherit her mother's disdain for sexual dalliance. She must have felt she had to live up to her name.

Aphrodite was the goddess of love, and I had three lovesick swains just dying to prove it.

The first thing that had to be done was to separate the love goddess from her amours. For sanitary reasons she was removed to the kitchen. Boo, much against her will, was also relegated to the kitchen to keep Aphrodite company. Boo took her revenge for the loss of the living room furniture by sulking in the center of the kitchen floor, hoping to trip anybody who didn't watch where he was going. Walter missed his access to the refrigerator. I suspected he was moaning as much over that as over Aphrodite.

Boo, because of her close association with the love goddess, lived a perilous existence. The few times she took a stroll among the amorous males she was immediately pounced upon. She cleaned house with them with the same fury she'd used on their father. After each episode they retired to nurse their injured male egos.

They completely lost interest in everything except what was out of their reach in the kitchen. I kept the TV going with all their favorite programs, but they couldn't sit still long enough to keep track of "Captain Kangeroo" or the new "Lost in Space" reruns. There were half-chewed chewies all over the floor from where they had started to eat but had spit them out when the chewing began to interfere with their howling and crying. About the only time they stopped their pacing was when they stepped on one of the chewies and it stuck to their feet and they had to dig it out from between their toes. They were a thoroughly miserable-looking crew.

The two in the kitchen weren't much better off. They missed their programs on TV. They didn't howl or moan piteously like the bunch in the living room, but they moped and their eyes followed my every move. It made me itchy to have four eyes fixed on me constantly. I wished they shared Walter's interest in the refrigerator. At least maybe they'd stare at it instead of me. To break the boredom, I hustled the family provider over to his mother's to borrow her extra, portable TV set.

"What do I tell Mom when she asks why we need her set?"

"Tell her the truth," I grunted, while I was making sure the barrier closing off the living room doorway was firmly in place.

"She won't believe that."

"Then tell her I've got a parakeet in the kitchen, and I'm trying to teach it to talk."

"God, we must have the weirdest dogs in the world," he said.

He brought the portable TV home, and Boo felt better.

Aphrodite didn't care. She was busy trying to chew her way through the plaster wall to the boys. It wasn't sisterly devotion.

Between raps on the backside, I screeched at her, "Stop chewing the walls, you harlot. You'll get your chance when I'm ready, and it won't be one of your brothers."

The pandemonium was without end. My world had turned into a nightmare of whining, mewling, and outright yowling. I got hoarse from screaming back at them. Every time I went near the fellows, they swooned at my feet.

"Take us to her, take us to her," they almost managed to talk.

"Stop that," I'd bellow at them. "Stop it before I pound your heads into mush."

Nothing was working. The nights were the worst.

For safety's sake, at bedtime we each took a male into our bedrooms. Apollo, being the brightest and the most likely to come up with a workable plan for an unwanted alliance, was kept in the master bedroom with two of us to keep watch. The kids drew lots and the younger won. She chose Stanley because he was the slowest of the three about sex and went to sleep without pacing the floor for an hour. Older daughter got stuck with Walter.

The first night of the new sleeping arrangements, I tried ignoring the din coming from the bedroom across from ours. I rolled over and squinted at the glowing green hands pointing to one-thirty. Oh Lordy.

The argument grew louder, and I waited for the shriek I knew was coming . . .

"Motherrrr! Would you pullease ask *your* dog to get out of my bed?"

I tried mashing the pillow over my head, but her voice could pierce a lead-lined room when she was aroused.

"Mother? Are you awake?"

"Yes!" I snarled through two closed doors.

"Then would you please come here and remove this dog?"

I hauled myself out of the bed, fell over Apollo, and banged my shin against the dresser drawer I'd forgotten to close.

105

"Damn," I moaned as I crossed the hall and confronted the complainant. I jumped on the offensive.

"Alright! Now I'm here. Shut up your screeching before you wake up the whole house."

"I tried to be nice, but you wouldn't answer," she mumbled back at me.

I continued pressing my offensive.

"Last winter, when it was cold, you were darned glad to have Walter sleeping with you."

"But he's got halitosis again. He keeps breathing on me," she said sullenly.

"Then turn your head the other way," I said.

"It won't help. He likes to watch me sleep."

"That's crazy," I said.

"Then watch him."

She demonstrated. She was right. I watched as Walter hoisted himself over her prone figure from side to side as she turned. It seemed to be her face that fascinated him.

"What do you have on your face?" I asked.

"That stuff that grandma gave me to make freckles go away."

"Of course, that's what he's after," I crowed triumphantly. "He likes the smell of your freckle cream."

"Then let's trade dogs. You take Walter and I'll take Apollo." Maybe she was right. Apollo might not care for freckle cream.

"Okay Walter," I said. "Come on, let's go to my room." Walter wouldn't move. He was reluctant to leave the freckle cream.

"Walter!" No movement. It was like the day at the vet's with the dead pigeon. "Walter!" Still nothing. Now I was waking up the whole house.

I started back across the hall doing my pussy cat imitation. Walter threw himself off the bed, clickety clicked his way across the hall in pursuit of the pussy cat and almost ran over Apollo. He banged into the bedroom, nosed around under my shoes and under the corners of the rug, and followed the telephone wire until he bumped into the wall. Walter was a dedicated pussy cat hater. Which was strange. In his entire life, Walter had never met a pussy cat face to face. He hadn't the foggiest notion of whether they swam, flew, or walked around on six legs. But he knew he hated pussy cats.

Walter's crashing around brought outraged complaints from the figure in the bed.

"What in God's name is he doing now?" he groaned from under the covers he'd pulled over his head to drown out the argument across the hall.

"He's hunting," I explained.

"Hunting!" He rose straight up in the bed. "At two in the morning? In the bedroom?" He was incredulous.

"He's hunting pussy cats," I said, as if there was nothing unusual about hunting pussy cats in the bedroom.

"He's got two minutes to catch and kill his pussy cat, or I will personally throw him out of the second-story window."

"Walter, honey," I coaxed, "come here and you can sleep with me."

Walter climbed up on my side of the bed and settled his head alongside mine on the pillow.

"Walter, close your eyes," I said. "You're making me nervous staring."

He closed his eyes.

"Walter," I whispered. "Tomorrow you go to the vet's. Your breath is gross, really gross."

W hen I woke up that morning, I knew something was different. Through the bedroom window a patch of sky was just beginning to signal that spring had arrived, at long last. It was a patch of the wispy blue, springtime sky that comes for the brief space of time between the cold, brittle blue of winter and the hot brassy blue of midsummer. The old pine tree outside the window still held some of its winter coating of snow, but I knew, I knew, I *knew* it was finally over.

I rolled over, slid my feet around searching for my battered scuffs, and headed down the stairs feeling excited for the first time since those first few snowflakes had begun sticking to my windshield.

Well, God, You finally made it back from the Bahamas, I thought. I flipped on the TV to "Spiderman" for the waiting group and headed for the kitchen and the daily battle with the half-dead toaster. Even a toaster that cooked the bread only on one side couldn't spoil my mood today. I leaned my chin on my cupped hand and almost believed I could see the hillside outside the window turning green. In a flush of springtime madness, I even took down from the front door the sign that said, "BATHROOM CLOSED UNTIL SPRING." The little hawks must have been watching all winter, because that afternoon my first returnee hit the door. It was my old myopic friend from last summer. Sometime over the winter, his vision must have improved. The glasses were thinner, and he didn't look like a startled owl anymore.

I still recognized the gravelly voice when he asked, "Did you really eat that yikky stuff?"

"We certainly did, and it was delicious."

"I wouldn't eat that stuff. YIK!" he said, screwing up his face in distaste.

"You didn't get invited for breakfast either, did you?" I undercut him.

He disappeared into the bathroom, and I hollered after him,"Take it easy on the paper, willya? Or you kids are going to have to start bringing your own."

"I don't use paper," gravel voice peeped through the closed door. He paused on his way out.

"I'm a boy," he said to me, as if I'd just left the convent day before yesterday. "Boys don't need paper."

I grinned as I watched him plodding down the driveway to wherever it was he came from behind the hill. I'd never tell him, but secretly I was glad he was back.

29

I drove onto the show grounds, parked the car, and coaxed Apollo from his perch on the back seat.

As we made our way toward the green-and-white-striped tents and the low wooden fences enclosing the freshly mowed grass, the air was soft and carried the smell of the fresh-turned earth of the surrounding fields. The sun was just beginning to chase the early morning chill.

It held the promise of one of those rare days when everything comes together for a dog show. We were back and it felt good.

I began feeling the familiar rush of emotion—the tightening in the chest, the shaky knees—and all the things I'd learned began rolling across my mind. You've got a fast-gaiting dog. Get to the front of the line. Don't get trapped behind some clunker. Don't string him up on the lead like a terrier and make him hackney in front. Pose him, and then *let him alone*. Don't drive the judge crazy fiddling around with him. He's got it all. Just let him look like the beautiful natural creature he is. Could I remember it all? I wondered. Practical things intruded. Should I make the long trek to the rest room now or wait until it was over? I damned that last cup of coffee. My mouth was so dry my tongue felt glued to my teeth. I was tempted to pop one of Apollo's chewies in my mouth, but then he'd want one, too, and then he'd dribble and then he'd get messy. I suffered with the dry mouth.

Apollo sat complacently at my feet, wagging his tail at passersby, trying to mooch some petting, and taking half-hearted swipes at a fly buzzing around him.

I looked around at the others gathered ringside with their expectant owners. I mentally assessed each of the other dogs' virtues and vices. I compared Apollo to each of them, ticked off

110

the ones who looked hopeless against him, and studied the one heart-stopper. He was a good dog. I couldn't kid myself. Point for point, sitting there waiting, they looked nearly equal. We were in for a fight for the points today.

It would take everything I'd learned. The shows where I'd nearly frozen in some unheated airplane hangar—dog shows are not always held in the best places—and the muggy heat of some bean patch in the middle of nowhere because there were no buidings large enough for a dog show. I thought back to crepe de chine Edna and her pink ribbons and naked angels and the patience of Boo while I learned. I blushed again at the remembrance of that first blue ribbon when somebody had to tap me and tell me I'd won. And the judge laughing. All of it, every bit of it, would always be worth those few brief moments when you tried and succeeded in proving you have the very best dog.

My reverie was broken by the voice of the ring steward calling our class. It was our turn. The other dog, the one I'd feared, moved toward the ring and my hopes rose. He was choppy in the rear. Apollo, with his effortless driving movement would win. Relief poured over me. Today was our day.

The judge smiled a lot. At everybody. We all did our thing and he watched and smiled, and touched the dogs and smiled, and moved us around the ring again and again and smiled. The sweat was pouring down underneath my thin cotton blouse, my legs felt mushy as I dropped to my knees and grasped Apollo's muzzle. He had to see what I already knew. Apollo had the most beautiful head of all the dogs in the ring. The wrinkles fell in velvety folds, the eyes were deeply set, and the skull was elegantly narrow. My hands shook as I tried to hold his head steady; I could barely breathe. The judge looked at Apollo, and Apollo gazed back at him gravely. The judge moved to his rear, and I crawled to the rear, making sure each foot was under him exactly where it should be. I leaned away, and Apollo stood on his own as if carved from marble. All those long hours of posing in the basement were paying off. I didn't have to hold onto him to cover up faults so the judge wouldn't find them. The tension mounted until I couldn't remember ever being anywhere else except in this grassy ring. I had never before seen a judge take so long to make a decision.

Fear was beginning to creep over me. I knew something was

wrong. He made Apollo and the dog I'd singled out as his only real competition move to the end of the row, and then he ignored us. I fought against the sense of foreboding that it wasn't going right. He gave the signal for us to begin moving in that last circuit of the ring that always comes before the decision, and I struggled to my feet. Apollo moved like the wind at my side. I could feel the power of his rear end driving his body forward as he skimmed over the grass. God how I loved him at that moment . . .

From far off I heard the judge's voice calling, one-two-three-four. I watched, dumbfounded, as the very worst dog in the ring and his owner plodded over to first place. Neither Apollo nor the dog that I'd worried over were even placed in the ribbons. Disbelief and then total rage swept over me. I was too mad to cry.

We made our way out of the ring blinded by anger and hurt. The ringsiders stood in shock. They knew, as I knew, that we had been the victims of the one thing that is the greatest threat to a wonderful sport—dishonest judges.

Ignorance or plain stupidity can be understood, but never this. And there is no appeal, no defense against such people, except never to show under them again. Everything in the sport of dogs is based on the ethics of each individual in it, and unfortunately there are always a few who ignore those ethics. All the American Kennel Club rules cannot regulate the moral standards of the few who lack a sense of decency and fair play.

Ringsiders tried to console, and it helped a little, but the bitter taste of a political defeat is sour in your mouth for a long time.

For the very first time, I really, honestly, wanted to quit.

The motel dining room was almost empty. I sat at a table in the corner, picking at the mashed potatoes with their pasty-tan gravy and the fatty chunk of beef that defied the knife when I tried to cut it. I was still too hurt to be hungry.

I remembered other judges who had sometimes made us winners and others who had not quite seen Apollo as the best dog on that day. I hated to lose, but I'd been able to believe they had done what they believed was right. Today was not one of those days.

More than anything else, I wanted to pile Apollo in the car and head for home. I was tired and lonely, and I wanted to be back in my home with my husband, my kids, and a room filled with fat rumps in a pile in front of the fireplace even if it was too warm for a fire. I didn't want to go back to an empty motel room.

"I wouldn't go home if I were you," a voice said.

I looked up at a figure standing beside my table. I'd seen him before at dog shows. A very large man with heavy Teutonic features that rarely showed emotion. Even on the hottest days, his jacket was neatly buttoned over his rotund figure. I'd been awed when I watched him show his dogs with an expertise I knew I'd never attain, no matter how long I worked at it.

It was easy for him to say that, I thought. When he walks in the ring, everyone knows who he is. He's not some little housewife with one good dog and a dream.

In the same voice I'd heard him use to urge his dogs to give that last ounce it took to win, he said to me now, "Today was a bad day. But it was only one day and one dog show."

I found my voice long enough to say bitterly, "But I should have won."

"Yes," he agreed with me. "Do you love your dog?" he asked.

"Yes."

"Do you believe you have a truly good dog?"

"Of course."

"Then don't go home. Don't quit."

He walked away with a curiously light tread for such a huge man.

I shoved the plate away and went back to the room.

I curled up in bed with Apollo beside me. It was a long time before I could fall asleep.

It was only one day and one dog show. I repeated his words to myself as I listened to Apollo snoring lightly beside me.

I would remember his words many more times during the good and the bad times that lay ahead.

30

Rain was pelting against the motel's windows as the seldom-used travel alarm clock's sound whirred through the room. When most of your traveling is done with small kids, you don't need alarm clocks. My legs were numb, and for a few seconds I panicked until I realized Apollo was sprawled across them. I thrust myself up like an athlete doing stomach tighteners and prodded him awake.

"Get off my legs, dummy, before I get gangrene," I hissed.

I punched the button down and silenced the alarm. Apollo rolled off my legs, stretched, and then went back to sleep.

I sat up in bed watching the beads of rain sliding down the window and thought seriously of pulling the covers over my head. To hell with another dog show. We'd sleep until a decent hour, eat breakfast, and roll for home. I was sliding back down under the covers when Apollo stood up, shook himself, and wagged his tail at me. He had to go out.

"For God's sake, can't you hold it for another hour?" I crabbed at him.

He wagged his tail harder and jumped down from the bed to prove he was serious.

"It's easy for you," I said. "You didn't cry yourself to sleep last night."

I pulled the old raincoat on over my pajamas, slid my bare feet into my shoes, and led him down the hall to the grass behind the motel. There, other half-asleep dog owners were standing around, glumly waiting for their early risers to pick a spot that suited them, get the job done, and then make a dash back inside.

Apollo was entranced with all the wonderful, strange odors. I yanked him from one fragrance to another trying to hurry him up.

"You're not out here to conduct a survey of canine elimina-
tions. Do it!" I commanded.

The rain was beginning to seep through the raincoat as we
tracked a Bloodhound bitch and her dripping owner to the
farthest limits of the motel's grass. Only after she'd finished and
he'd thoroughly checked the spot did he finally do what he'd
insisted to me in the room was a disaster in the making if I
didn't move pronto.

He curled up on the bed again while I unrolled the curlers
from my hair, a useless gesture since three minutes outside and
it would be nothing but a headful of limp strings. I repacked the
new skirt and blouse that had been intended for my victory
celebration if we won and pulled the raincoat back on over
yesterday's outfit. With an old rain scarf tied babushka-style
around my head, I looked like a Ukrainian refugee in an old
World War II picture.

Today's show site was fifty miles in the opposite direction
from yesterday's beautiful university athletic field. I cringed at
the muddy mess I knew lay ahead of us. We drove behind
eighteen-wheelers slewing up mud on the two-lane road. I
checked the time, speeded up, passed, checked the time, and
then settled back behind another eighteen-wheeler slewing up
more muddy water from the pavement. I never knew so many
trucks rolled on Sunday.

Apollo leaned his head against me as I drove; he felt warm
and trusting, and it took away some of the loneliness. Overhead
the clouds turned dirtier and grayer, and I wished I had gone
home. It was only one day and one dog show. There would be
others.

The show grounds were a solid sea of mud. No tents, no
banners flying in the breeze, like yesterday. Only mud and ring
fences wobbling unsteadily in a wet wind blowing sheets of rain
across the open field. In this ocean of mud, what could I expect
of Apollo? I looked around to see if my friend from last night was
there. I had a few things I would have liked to mention to him,
especially my thoughts right now about his advice not to go
home.

We huddled around the Basset ring in a dreary group,
sharing our misery and cups of lukewarm coffee. I looked
around for yesterday's winner. In today's gook, even flopfoot
from yesterday might look good. He was absent. I asked one of
my companions where he was. It was no surprise when I heard

115

he was one of those called "spot showers." This meant he was only shown under judges who didn't know as much as they should about a breed, or the few like yesterday's politician.

The judge today watched us grave-faced and unsmiling. His eyes never left the dogs as he struggled to see each of them. He seemed impervious to the pouring rain as he put us through our paces.

Apollo moved without breaking his stride, spewing up jets of water as his feet hit and then reaching for the next step. I stumbled and nearly fell, regained my balance, and cursed under my breath. For a brief moment I thought back to Boo and that first day I saw her in that muddy barnyard. No wonder this idiot doesn't mind, I thought. He takes after his mother.

It seemed to be taking forever, while the judge examined each dog carefully, gaited us alone, then moved back and forth along the line of dogs, always searching with eyes that seemed to see beneath the fur and to the muscles and bone structure. We were all equal in his eyes. He raised his hand and gave the signal that sent us on that last heart-stopping circuit around the ring. Dogs and people forgot the mud and the rain and the bad judges. It was another day and another dog show. He pointed to us and uttered the magic words, "First Place," and we swung out of the line and stood before the marker with number one painted on it.

One more step remained before those precious two points were ours. The winners from the other classes came back, but I knew deep in my heart Apollo couldn't lose that day. The judge pointed once more and said, "Winner's Dog"; and it wasn't just another day and another dog show for me.

I wasn't ashamed of the tears as he handed me the ribbon. Later, I would learn to accept it with more aplomb, but I never learned to accept one casually.

Through a cloud of happiness, I heard the ring steward asking me, "Do you want a picture?"

Did I want a picture! I didn't even remember that I looked like a Ukrainian refugee or that Apollo was mud splattered and water was running off him in rivulets.

"Of course, I want a picture!" I said. And for the very first time I could give voice to my dream, "This finished him today. He's a CHAMPION."

And my heart sang.

31

The old house was quiet with the stillness of a midsummer night.

Upstairs the matching outfits for tomorrow night's piano recital hung alongside each girl's bed. Good grief, I wondered, how many more times would they play the same duet. If they tried any funny stuff tomorrow night—like the last time, when one of them had held the other's keys down—I'd kill both of them.

The family provider's light snores drifted down the stairway. I'd have to roll him over pretty soon, before he went under too deep.

But for now, I sat and let contentment wrap itself around me. I had climbed my mountain, and tonight I was filled with the satisfaction of having kept the promise I had made to myself—to breed a champion of my own. In the future there would be other mountains to climb, and between the mountain tops there would be other whelping boxes, more Pablum, more puddles, and more chewed furniture. There would be more Walters and Stanleys and Aphrodites with hearts filled with love, but never quite the stuff of which a show dog is made. They would have their place and be as loved as any champion. There would always be room for one more dog. On the mountain would be other things as well. Stretching ahead were still years of sewing yards and yards of Lady Guinevere court dresses and nylon net tutus for my two left-footed Margot Fonteyns asleep upstairs. Dinner parties when the dogs would have to be expelled from the house and would sit staring mournfully through the windows at strangers sitting on *their* furniture. Endless explanations to friends who couldn't understand anyone who wanted to own more than one dog. My mother-in-law who would never tire of

telling me about all the beautiful things I could have, if I just didn't waste all that money feeding a bunch of dogs. But the people who really counted, my family, knew and understood. That was all that really mattered. They would always be there to cheer me at the top of the mountain.

As I sat on the old couch, absorbed in reverie, my eyes kept sliding across the room to the silver bowl glinting in the light from the lamps. Champion Apollo's bowl sat proudly among Boo's naked angels. I had made my dream come true.

I looked at the pile where Champion Apollo was half-buried under Walter and Stanley. Walter was dribbling again.

"Walter, would you please stop drooling chewie spit on his head. You're making him sticky," I said for the umpteenth time.

Walter responded by licking the chewie dribble and liked the taste so well that he pinned Apollo's head down with one of his bear paws and cleaned the champ's entire head. The stickiness made his fur stand up like a porcupine. I wished I had just kept quiet.

Stanley, disgusted with the steady slopping sounds of Walter's licking, unwound himself from the pile and climbed up on the couch beside me. He dropped his massive head in my lap, and his soft brown eyes looked straight into mine. Only one of them would ever be a champion to the dog world, but to me they were all winners.

"Come on, group. Everybody on your feet. Let's get going."

The moon was a chalk ball riding high in the summer sky as they poked around in the grass. I watched as they did their duty and then waited for Boo to lead them back inside. She stood alone with the moonlight gleaming on her coat, her eyes looking out across the empty fields. We all waited for her. To these her children, and to all the others still to come, she would always be the grande dame.